Richard Waldo Sibthorp

Daily Bread

being a few morning meditations for the use of Catholic Christians

Richard Waldo Sibthorp

Daily Bread

being a few morning meditations for the use of Catholic Christians

ISBN/EAN: 9783742865069

Manufactured in Europe, USA, Canada, Australia, Japa

Cover: Foto ©Lupo / pixelio.de

Manufactured and distributed by brebook publishing software (www.brebook.com)

Richard Waldo Sibthorp

Daily Bread

DAILY BREAD:

BEING A

FEW MORNING MEDITATIONS

FOR THE

USE OF CATHOLIC CHRISTIANS.

IMPRIMATUR:

EDUARDUS, Episcopus Nottinghamiensis.

ADVERTISEMENT.

THE Meditations now published under the Title of DAILY BREAD, consist of a few Discourses, in part delivered at the weekly Morning Service of the Mass, in St. Barnabas Cathedral, Nottingham. They were necessarily short, not to interfere with the worldly callings of those who attended. It was desired that these might take away something to keep in mind, in their various occupations, with their families, and throughout the day: something to aid them, by the Divine Blessing, to fulfil the Apostles' exhortation: *Building yourselves upon your most holy faith, praying in the Holy Ghost; keep yourselves in the love of God, waiting for the mercy of our Lord Jesus Christ unto life everlasting.*

They are published, confessedly also, with a hope that some who read them may prayerfully remember, when it shall please God to close his earthly pilgrimage, him who in the few last years of a protracted life, helped others to minister to them the Word of God, and the Sacraments of the Church.

Their friend and servant,

RICHARD WALDO SIBTHORP.

East Circus Street, Nottingham,
    January, 1876.

N.B.—The quotations from Holy Scripture are, with scarcely an exception, from the authorized Douay version of the Bible.

ERRATA.

Page 3, line 3, for "consequently," read "invariably."
,, 10, ,, 6, for "thoughful," ,, "thoughtful."
,, 32, ,, 1, for "head," ,, "heart."
,, ,, 13, for "become," ,, "becomes."
,, 47, ,, 24, for "them," ,, "Him."
,, 74, ,, 1, for "am," ,, "a."
,, 130, ,, 1, for "Catholics," ,, "Catholic."
,, ,, 5, for "faith," ,, "life."
,, 131, ,, 12, omit "for," after "did."
,, 136, ,, 18, for "our," read "own."
,, 151, ,, 7, after "soul," supply "is."

"DAILY BREAD."

1.

IT is well to remember each morning that your Heavenly Father is now calling you to your lawful employment, whatever it be. For you *are the people of his hand and the sheep of his pasture.* Therefore go forth in dependence upon His loving guidance, watchful care, and sustaining help—expect His blessing. Look to Him, that your souls may be somewhat more filled this day with His grace, and your spirits refreshed with a sufficiency of the peace of God. Not only enter on it, but continue, in prayer; As you have time and opportunity, meditate on useful and holy things. Seek to hear edifying words, and nourish profitable thoughts in your hearts; desire a clearer apprehension of God, His character, truth, and love to you in Christ; nor be cast down if it is otherwise, but expect a more unclouded and lightsome to-morrow. Keep faith and hope in exercise. Offer yourselves to God, with cheerful submissiveness of heart, to be both as to soul and body a living sacrifice, mindful of what the Church daily reminds you, that you are not only the Lord's servants, but likewise

His holy people. Look on this day as granted you for the work of getting ready for eternity. Commence it by fastening yourselves in spirit to Christ's cross. There is no safer or more honorable position for you to be in.

2.

St. Paul wrote of himself, what is true of each of us, *when I am weak then am I strong*, *i.e.*, when I am filled with a sense of my own weakness, and finding my utter helplessness, put a simple and entire confidence in God, then I am strong in the power of His might. *I can do all things, through Christ, which strengtheneth me.* On the other hand, it is not less true, that when we are strong in our own conceits, then we are most weak. When we fancy ourselves able to bear, and do all things of ourselves, and confide, or even, as we are prone to, glory in our own supposed spiritual strength, then is the time of our utter weakness. For God withholds His support from presumption, and we are left deservedly to ourselves. Let us never lose sight, then, of the fact that our own strength is absolute weakness, as to spiritual efficiency and progress; dependence on it tends only to humiliating failures and grievous falls; while conscious weakness, with a lowly spirit of confidence in God, is our true strength; God's own strength is then perfecting in us *whatsoever things are holy, lovely, and of good fame.* Take this as a lesson for a daily Christian life, that we walk securely only as we walk humbly. St. Peter had to learn this lesson, and let his denial of his Master teach it to us.

3.

They who have most opportunities of learning what Christ requires of them, by no means always profit most. Religious advantages do not consequently lead to the most sound, advanced, and enlightened piety. We learn from the Gospels that a centurion who was most probably brought up in heathenism, and became a convert to the faith and worship of the Jews, showed a stronger faith in Christ than the Ruler of the Jewish Synagogue, who had grown up from his youth in acquaintance with the law of Moses, and God's commandments, and gracious dealings with His people. For this Centurion did not ask the Lord to go to his house to heal his sick servant, but while yet at a distance to *speak the word only*, and the cure would follow; while the Jewish Ruler said *Come and lay Thy hand upon her and she shall live*. He would have the Lord to go with him to his house, which, in His condescending love, Christ did, stooping thus, in His meek and lowly mind, to human infirmity. Let us learn hence to be watchful over the use of our Christian knowledge, and means of grace, that they produce the good fruits of faith and humility in our daily conduct and conversation, and that *we may adorn in all things the doctrine of God our Saviour*, which we have learned and profess. Let us especially beware of letting any conceit of our own merit, in the sight of God, find place, as it easily does, in our hearts. It was well written:

> Jesus cast a look on me,
> Give me sweet simplicity;
> Make me poor, and keep me low,
> Seeking only Thee to know.

Make me like a little child,
Of my strength and wisdom spoiled;
Seeing only in Thy light,
Walking only in Thy might.

4.

We are not always willing to accept the fact of our own nothingness, and the necessity of a daily dying unto self. Yet God, in requiring such self humiliation, would only have us to bring home to ourselves our true position. It is well for us to distrust ourselves. Alas! how often particular and great failings remind us of what we are, and what we should be, if left to ourselves. How easily, for instance, sloth gets the better of our resolutions and convictions. How soon after our morning's devotions we become indolent, waste time, do our work, whether for God or man, partially, negligently, and with an inward, or manifest, distaste for it. We often go to public and private prayer unwillingly, and move from it gladly, as if our hearts said, *Behold our labour*. When we have done little for God, and His Church, and Truth, we think much of it; as if we had made God our debtor, forgetting that we are *unprofitable servants* at the best. In fact, indolence and irresolution, and weariness, in what is good, beset most of us. Good Catholics had often rather read pious books, than work good works; they had rather sit and meditate at home on sacred things and Church news, than go out and about neighbourly duties. We seek and find out numerous excuses for easing our necks of the yoke of self-denial. But all true peace lies in a forgetfulness of self, which can only be found in a thorough, hearty, continuous surrender to God, His service, and known will. Once gain this, and neither earth nor hell will much prevail to trouble you, or disturb your rest in Him, and your perseverance in a godly life.

> O, how slowly have I often
>   Followed where Thy hand would draw!
> How Thy kindness fail'd to soften!
>   How Thy chastening fail'd to awe!
> Make me for Thy rest more ready,
>   As Thy path is longer trod.
> Keep me in Thy friendship steady,
>   Till Thou call me home, my God!

3.

It was God's condemnation of the ancient Heathens that they loved and served the creature more than the Creator. And is not this too true of ourselves? Does not some present thing, some pursuit of gain, of amusement, or worldly advantage of some kind, have more of our hearts, our time, thoughts, and care, than God? If we watch over ourselves we shall daily find that God has less of our service than this poor world, and what it brings before us. If our Saviour should put to us the question he put to St. Peter, *lovest thou me more than these?* can we truly say, *Lord, thou knowest all things, thou knowest that I love Thee.* If we are only conscious of our want of love of God, humbled that we serve him so poorly, earnest and persevering in prayer that we may serve Him better, and honest in our endeavour to do so, our Heavenly Father will, for Christ's sake, bear with us, help us on, lift us up from our falls, and perfect His strength in our weakness. Let this be a prospect of faith to cheer us, when cast down with our consciousness of our little faith, feeble hope and defective charity. Endeavour to keep your hearts fixed on God, and to see Him in all things; to love and serve the Creator with sincerity of heart more than the creature; say to yourself,

> Renouncing every worldly thing,
> Safe 'neath the covert of Thy wing,
> My sweetest thought henceforth shall be,
> That all I want I find in Thee,
> In Thee,
> My God, in Thee.

6.

Pardoning love is a character in which God delights to manifest Himself to us: *forgiving iniquity, transgression, and sin.* The debt of guilt we have contracted in our lives, even the young who are here, is immense. We have need, as we also have the fullest encouragement, to pray daily, *forgive us our trespasses.* But let us not forget, what we add to that petition; *as we forgive them that trespass against us.* The unforgiving servant in the Gospel stirs our indignation as we hear it read, but is it not a too faithful representation of very many among ourselves? We deal out to our fellow servants, our brethren in Christ, a different measure from that of God to us. He pardons our many and great offences, and throughly on our true penitence. We are apt to be unforgiving of every slight offence against what we consider our rights; we forgive reluctantly, and with reserve; seldom fully, freely, and heartily. Often when we profess to forgive one who has offended or injured us, we retain a coldness of heart and a distance of manner scarcely differing from retained hatred, or, at best, dislike.

What room for daily amendment of our spirit, and improvement of our conduct, may we find as to this matter! Remember, that our loving God observes our want of love. Nor forget that *this commandment have we from God, that he who loveth God, love his brother also.* There are few defects in Christians more observable than an unforgiving spirit.

7.

The holy Psalmist prays—*Let not the oil of the sinner fatten my head.* That oil is often flattery. It will be true wisdom to watch against, and to pray to be delivered from it. The Pharisees, when they took counsel to entangle Jesus in his speech, sought to succeed by flattery. *Master*, they said, *we know that thou art a true speaker, and teachest the way of God in truth, neither carest thou for any man.* Flattery is not always falsehood; but sometimes truth, as in our Lord's case, but spoken with a bad purpose; and the danger is scarcely less, when the purpose is not bad. When honestly spoken, and from true affection, it will act as a poison, helping to feed and flatter self-esteem in the hearer, than which nothing can be more hurtful, or more retard spiritual progress. The kingdom of heaven is for the *poor in spirit.* If we know ourselves, we must be conscious that we want no flattery to make us think well of ourselves, and *not wise to sobriety.* It may be taken as an invariable rule of God in dealing with those He loves, to keep down self-esteem, to humble them, and stablish His kingdom within them, on the breaking up of that dangerous occupant of our hearts. Flattery opposes this plan of God for our good. Let us neither receive it for ourselves, nor use it to others. The wise King of Israel says—*A man that speaketh to his friend with flattering and dissembling words, spreadeth a net for his feet;* and St. Paul says of himself, what we shall do well to keep in mind, *neither have we used at any time the speech of flattery.*

8.

Sanctification or personal holiness is not the work of a day; it involves the conflict of the whole life. We have to fight, not as they *who beat the air,* but as having mighty adversaries within and without, to resist and overcome. There is a danger against which we require to be warned; the regarding, with any approval, the evil we see in others. We must be careful not to thus consent to any who do or say what God has given us the light to understand to be sinful. We need not, at any time, be sourly austere; it may seldom be our duty to reprove, but we must neither by look, word, or act, give cause to suppose that we acquiesce in what offends God. It shows a weak mind to take offence at little things that may not be perfectly correct, and it is a mistake to consider what is not to be approved of, as our own fault, whether we have or not consented. And it shows want of judgment, and wrong zeal, to rebuke everything deserving of rebuke that we hear or see; but it is very needful to keep watch over our own hearts, lest they catch the taint of evil that comes to us through our eyes or ears, and so bring it home to our souls. *Be ye holy,* God says, *for I am holy,* and *without holiness no man shall see God.*

There is a restraint of silence and of look, which often rebukes sin as effectually as an outspoken reproof, and commonly with less danger to the rebuked and the rebuker. *There is a time to keep silence and a time to speak.*

9.

Christ, in taking our nature upon Him, engaged to sympathize with us. Almost every creature is tender towards its kind, however ferocious to others. The savage bear will not be deprived of her cubs without resistance, but will tear the intruder to pieces if she can. How great must be the jealousy of our loving God and Lord for us His children! He will not be deprived easily of any of them. Having taken them to be His own members, for we are such, He watches over them with tenderest care. How much will a man do, and bear, before he suffers one of his bodily members to be cut off! Think not that any one of us would do more to preserve his own members than our Lord will do for us. In all things, the pre-eminence is His. He is acquainted with all our temptations, having been *once tempted in all things like as we are, without sin.* Are you, then, tempted to deny or forget God? So was Christ. Are you tempted to prefer the world's favour to God? So was Christ. Are you tempted by the world's vanities? So was He. Are you tempted to please and serve the devil? So was He. From His birth in the stable of Bethlehem, to His death on the cross, He was tempted; and He, our divine head in heaven, sympathizes now with us—His feet pinched and pressed on earth. Shall not *that mind be in us which was in Christ Jesus?* There is great consolation and weighty instruction in our Lord's sympathy with us. For ought not we to sympathize with our fellow-creatures, and Christians, in their trials and sorrows; as one writes beautifully—

> I ask Thee for a thoughful love,
>   Through constant watching wise;
> To meet the glad with joyful smiles,
>   And wipe the weeping eyes.
> And a heart at leisure from itself,
>   To soothe and sympathize.

10.

The soul of man is barren and unfruitful till the Word of God comes down upon it like the rain from heaven, and it is watered with the dew of His life-giving grace. When but a little sprinkling of the latter enters and softens it, what a rich crop of graces, and what a harvest of good works will be produced. Is your heart so full of malice and hatred that the most humble suppliant can expect no forgiveness? Is it so full of revenge and wrath that the roaring sea, agitated by a tempest, is more easy to be calmed and made still? Is it so penurious and fond of money, that no wretched object, no call of charity, can get a penny from its grip? Is it so wanton, impure, and profligate that it is glad *when evil is done, and rejoices in wicked things?* Yet, when the Spirit of God comes with the Word of God upon it, the stone will be turned to flesh, the tumultuous sea hushed into calm, the *mountains of Gilboa*, barren and scorched, become *fields of first-fruits.* Mark some of the recorded changes— Zaccheus, the greedy publican and hard-hearted tax gatherer, *restores four-fold what he had wronged any man of, and gives half of his goods to the poor.* Saul, the persecutor, becomes from an enemy, raging like a wild beast against them, gentle as a lamb, and loving to *the disciples of the Lord Jesus.* The careless heathen, Felix, trembles like an aspen leaf, as the apostle speaks before him of *justice, and chastity, and the judgment to come.* Peter leaves his boats and his fishing nets to *catch men* in the net of the gospel. *He that hath ears to hear let him hear,* with earnest, persevering *prayer, that the gospel may be to him, not in word only, but in power also, and in the Holy Ghost, and in much fulness,* for the converting, renovating grace of Christ is the same as ever, and not less needed by us now than of old time.

11.

True and saving religion is not so much a knowledge of God and of divine things as the life of God in the soul of man. Everything is best and most known by what best and most resembles it, and therefore so much stress is laid in Holy Scriptures on a truly Christian life; and our Lord says, *He that hath my commandments and keepeth them, he it is that loveth me.* True religion comes from the eternal light even from Him who says of himself *I am the light of the world,* and therefore, like the sunbeam, it not only enlightens but warms and enlivens. St. Paul, opening out the right way of becoming *wise unto salvation,* says *knowledge puffeth up, but charity edifieth.* That Christianity which is only learnt from creeds and confessions of faith, is but a poor, weak light; but the powerful working of a true and saving knowledge of God and of Christ within the soul by the Holy Ghost, shows itself in purity of heart and life. Therefore our Lord says, *Blessed are the clean of heart, for they shall see God.* Seek God and your Saviour, then, in your own souls, for that is the best, the truest, and only saving knowledge of Him, which is kindled within our hearts by the heavenly warmth of the Holy Spirit. Of this knowledge we are to understand Christ's words, *This is eternal life, that they may know Thee, the only true God, and Jesus Christ whom Thou hast sent.* For this, as a present, a daily, and hourly salvation, *ask and it shall be given you, seek and you shall find, knock and it shall be opened to you.* The promise is express, that God will give the Holy Spirit to them who ask.

12.

Set it down in your own minds, as a most certain truth, that sin and vice have a stupefying influence on the heart; they are like that fish which in some southern seas is said to benumb those who meddle with it. Besides other reasons for it there is this, that God Himself seems to us very often to be as we ourselves are. *Thou thoughtest unjustly that I shall be like to thee,* is His own word. There are many whose better judgments are smothered by their own evil appetites and worldly aims. Like light buried in some thick or dark body, their views of God, of Christ, of salvation, and of all gracious and saving things are discoloured and darkened by their own vices. So long as we harbour any besetting sin, whether it be profligacy or worldliness, no gracious or Christian dispositions will take root in our hearts. They may, like flowers plucked in a garden, and stuck in a pot of earth, show an outward beauty for a time, but soon wither and pass away. Sin sucks up the affections from God; carries captive the will, and fulfils in those who yield to it Christ's very solemn words, *You are of your father, the devil, and the desires of your father you will do.* But be *subject to God, and resist the devil, and he will flee from you: draw nigh to God and He will draw nigh to you. Cleanse, ye sinners, and purify your hearts, ye doubleminded.* In the strength of the Holy Spirit resist every wrong inclination you find rising in you. Consider how God says to you: *Be ye holy, for I the Lord your God am holy:* and that Jesus shed His blood on the cross for you, and has left for you that gracious, weighty declaration: *For them do I sanctify myself, that they also may be sanctified in truth.* Walk to-day in the light of it, praying that it may be your portion, and God will bless and keep you.

13.

There is a knowledge of *the truth, as it is in Jesus,* and as it is in every Christ-like nature, in that sweet, mild, humble and loving spirit of our Divine Lord, which spreads itself, like the beams of the morning sun, on some fair outlying fields, in the souls of true Christians, full of light and life. It profits little, we need to be often reminded, to know Christ in creeds and profession of faith, and in forms and outward devotion; but to have His Holy Spirit who *searcheth all things, yea, the deep things of God*, at work within our hearts, is of value beyond words to express. There is an inward power, life and beauty in divine truth, which cannot be fully known by us till we digest it into the daily life and practice. We may talk of God, and Christ, but they are only names, dry and profitless words, till they are unfolded in our hearts and lives in their significancy to us, and our spiritual needs. Observe how our Lord himself tested true acquaintance with the Gospel and salvation in doing God's will: *If any man will do the will of Him, he shall know of the doctrine, whether it be of God;* this is what alone will make us, as St. Peter says, *to be neither empty, nor unfruitful in the knowledge of our Lord Jesus Christ.* Be assured that a sensual heart and a worldly mind cannot relish the excellency and sweetness of Divine truth: that truth says, *The sensual man perceiveth not these things that are of the Spirit of God, for it is foolishness to him, and he cannot understand, because it is spiritually examined.* Corrupt passions, and worldly affections, warp our understandings, mislead our judgments, and disturb holy and calm thoughts. See what your first care in the morning should be, and your most earnest prayer in the day: *Create a clean heart in me, O God, and renew a right spirit within me.* Beware of *a form* of godliness without the power.

14.

It was Moses' complaint respecting the people of Israel in the wilderness, that *they provoked Him* (i.e., God), *by strange gods.* We are not likely to fall into this sin, nor that of the ancient Heathen who changed *the glory of the incorruptible God, into the likeness of the image of a corruptible man, and of birds, and four-footed beasts, and creeping things.* But most of us are ready to set up an idol in our hearts; some sin, or wrong temper, or worldly attachment. We must watch carefully, and pray perseveringly against this idolatry. Our God is *a jealous God.* He demands from us our whole hearts. Jesus came from Heaven to get them for God, and he observes us daily, hourly, and closely, to see how it is with us, His professing people. It is a chief design of Redemption as regards us. Christ honoured his Father, and would have us honour Him according to His own requirements. Try then to keep in mind, in all the circumstances of this day on which you now enter, in its duties, trials, and intercourse with others, that you are the creatures and servants of the Most High, true, and Holy God. Think well on what a great and awful Being He is, and render Him a loving, faithful, conscientious service. Walk by faith, and He will be faithful to all his promises to you. Love Him, and you will be loved by Him. Be careful not to let any wrong affection, or care, or pursuit have that place in your heart which God claims when he says, *Thou shalt not have strange gods before me. Little children,* writes St. John, *keep yourselves from idols.* Our idols are set up within our souls.

15.

Let us be careful not to give way to sadness ; still more, as some very sincere Christians are apt to, not to cherish it. A child of God, sheltered in the bosom of His eternal love, under the care of Jesus, ever full of tenderest sympathy, and in the guidance of the Holy Spirit, should have much abiding comfort, and be thankfully cheerful. We should reject, as temptations of the enemy of our souls, gloomy and desponding suggestions and thoughts, for he stirs up such within us, to harass, perplex, and weary. *Rejoice in the Lord always*, writes St. Paul to the Philippian believers, *and again I say, rejoice*, and repeatedly so in the same words. But, observe, that no grace tends more to keep us cheerful than humility, joined with gentleness, and recollection of our own sinfulness and unprofitableness. These are great fruits of the Holy Spirit in God's children, and which He fails not to bless us in the cultivation of, and when we fail in them, as, alas, we do very, very often, let us not then be cast down and dejected in spirit, and give way to sadness, but rise up again, in simple faith, and go on in our proper callings and Christian duties, as regards God and our neighbour. This will aid us to keep up a blessed sanctifying union with our dear Lord through the day. Go forth, then, now, keeping this in mind—*The Lord of peace himself give you everlasting peace in every place.* It is a good rule for avoiding sadness ourselves, to set about some endeavour to make a fellow Christian happier in Christ, even more comfortable as to this life.

16.

Some persons talk against what is called experience in religion. Do not join in with them. Enquire this of yourselves, and not seldom, if you find your affections drawing off from the world and its vanities (not to say from any sin and love of it) to Christ. Do you find in yourselves the working of the Spirit of Christ, mortifying the flesh, and its works, and drawing up your minds to better, and heavenly things? If so, doubt not that it is the work of God the Holy Ghost, who dwelleth in you, and give Him the glory of it. And as you prize communion with God, and value the teaching and comfort of the Holy Ghost, seek to be found daily in God's ways, in the highway of humble faith and obedient love, sitting much in spirit at the feet of Christ, and drinking in (so to speak) those sweet and sanctifying communications of His grace, which are at once an earnest of, and a preparation for, eternal life. Let us never think lightly of such experience as this in ourselves, nor be ashamed modestly to own it, nor offended with others, if reverently they speak of it. We find holy David saying—*Come and hear all ye that fear God, and I will tell you what great things He has done for my soul.* There must be *experience* of the love of God, of the value of Christ, and all this to us, and of the sanctifying work of the Holy Comforter, in every earnest Christian, and there are occasions when it is not unbecoming, but fitting, to speak of it. To disregard, or deride this, is to insult God, and it is to grieve the Holy Spirit if we keep His work shut up in our hearts. *We believe* (writes St. Paul), *for which cause we speak also.*

17.

Who hath despised little days (asks the Lord by the Prophet Zechariah), the day of small things. *Be* strengthened in the Lord, and in the might of His power, and as David says of his enemies, so we, feeble and corrupt as we are, and often seeming as if we had scarcely set forth to any purpose in the way to Heaven, may say of our temptations and spiritual difficulties: *They surrounded me like bees, and they burned like fire among thorns, and in the name of the Lord I was revenged on them.* Only let us set ourselves, with all our might, and a steady resolution, to mortify the old man, and to crucify all the wrong affections of the flesh, *laying aside every weight and sin which surrounds us, let us run by patience to the fight proposed to us; looking on Jesus, the author and finisher of faith, who is set down at the right hand of the throne of God*, as a great and mighty conqueror, who will shew the perfection of His own power in our weakness, if we lay hold on His strength. With confidence apply to him, who is an Almighty Saviour, and when He joins His strength with us, with our weakness, we need not fear anything. We shall break the old serpent's head, though he may bruise our heel. He, the compassionate, loving Jesus, does not despise our *little days.* It is written of Him: *He shall deliver the poor from the mighty, and the needy that hath no helper; their name shall be honourable in His sight.*

> Oft in trouble and in woe,
> Onward, Christians, onward go,
> Fight the fight, maintain the strife,
> Strengthened with the Bread of Life.

18.

True personal religion, which it is most needful to cherish, comes from Heaven, and moves towards Heaven again. *Every best and perfect gift is from above, coming down from the Father of Lights, with whom is no change, nor shadow of alteration, for of His own will hath He begotten us by the word of truth, that we might be some beginning of His creature.* True religion is a flowing out of the truth and goodness of God on the souls of men, and therefore they who have it are said to be *partakers of the Divine nature.* None but the highest of created beings can enjoy it. To be a true Christian is to be *born again*—or *from above.* All earthly nobility has its descent but from Adam, *the slime of the earth;* but a Christian as such derives his life from Christ, *the brightness of the glory of God, and the figure of His substance;* and it may truly be said of Christ, and true Christians, what was said of Gideon's brethren, *they were like thee, and one of them as the son of a king.* Titles of worldly honour are but nominal and temporary, but those by which God distinguishes his children declare what is real and lasting; as St. John observes: *Behold what manner of charity the Father has bestowed upon us, that we should be called and should be the sons of God.* Let God, therefore, have your hearts and wills, and a firm resolution built upon the strength of Christ that your religion shall be real, personal, practical; and let your daily prayer be, *Give me understanding, and I will search thy law, and I will keep it with my whole heart.*

19.

If we are truly influenced by our religion, we shall live much above the world and worldly gratifications. The soul is too powerful and noble when restored to its possession of the life offered, to be shut up in the prison of bodily and sensual enjoyments. It will ascend towards God, its original, and to immortality. It seems, as one of old said, "to be ashamed to be in the body;" or as St. Paul writes: *we groan, being burdened, that what is mortal may be swallowed up by life. He who maketh us for this very thing, is God, who hath given us the pledge of His spirit.* Rest assured that it is religion only which enables us to die to this world, and earthly things, the rendering of which is to darken our minds, and obscure in them the light of Christ. The proper movement of true godliness in us is to its first original: while ungodly men are really burying their souls in their bodies, their aims and desires, bounded within the world they inhabit. This is a living death of the saddest kind. Let us endeavour to look on ourselves, not by the attachment of the body and of this life, the cords which fasten us down, like the fabled man, to the earth, but by those of our renewed souls; for is not this the apostles advice? *Mind the things that are above; not the things that are upon the earth, for you are dead, and your life is hid with Christ in God.* Gather hence a noble aim of your daily life, however humble may be its present occupation. *Serve ye the Lord Christ.* A Christian, having the Holy Spirit in him, is not one whose soul is a servant, to wait upon his senses, and to be led up and down against sound reason, as well as sound religion, which is the condition of numbers around. He is called and enabled to converse and *walk with* God: to know and love Him, and to become more and more like Him. Oh! great distinction and most blessed privilege!

Keep it ever in mind; try to embody it into your daily life —*walk before me,* God says to each of us, *and be thou perfect.*

20.

Quietness and gentleness are graces, or become to us gracious habits, which we shall do well carefully to cherish. Especially if we are naturally active, lively, and quick, we should try to be under the influence of these graces in the common duties of the day. Let us sit down quietly to our meals, and take the food we need without hurry or eagerness. In some of the monastic religious houses, the broth and drink were and are taken in a kind of two-handled cup or basin, which prevented haste and eagerness in drinking it. When we go to bed, let us undress quietly, and get up in the morning calmly, without hurry and needless disquieting of others. In all the various matters of daily life, and in all our intercourse with others, let us check our tendency to be in a hurry and bustle, and try to be composed and gentle; and, as if our Lord was observing and near us. The want of this was a failing of pious Martha, overmuch *busy about much serving.* If we are naturally indolent, suppose Him saying to us, "make haste, for time is precious;" but if we are naturally quick and hasty, let us hear Him reminding us "Do not be in such a hurry, *so careful and troubled.*" Peace and calm of mind are really very precious attainments of a Christian. The Holy Spirit abides with calm and quiet spirits, as doves like to sit upon and shaded by still branches, and not on such as are tossed about by winds; *know you not that you are the temple of God, and the Spirit of God dwelleth in you?* In your daily course in this troubled and troublous world, keep this in mind, and you will find it a rest to your spirits.

21.

The keeping in mind the life of Jesus, and His passion and death, will, with God's gracious help, tend greatly to cherish in us a spirit of patience in the endurance of trials. The number is indeed past numbering of those who, keeping before them *the Crucified,* have been sustained in pain and comforted in bereavements; and who after disturbance of spirit through human infirmity, have been brought back to peace, and trustful love, and calm perseverance in a devout and holy life. It is not the mere contemplation of a crucifix, without the bringing home to our hearts and minds the calm and holy will of Christ, His joy in God, His endurance of sorrow past our comprehension, and life and death agony extreme that will benefit us. We must keep in remembrance how He said: *Take my yoke upon you, and learn of me, because I am meek and humble of heart, and you shall find rest to your souls.* Let us endeavour through the day to hear His warning voice of tender love, as saying to us, amid all our trials: *In your patience you shall possess your souls.* He is coming again to gather all His faithful ones to His and their heavenly home. *Be patient, and strengthen your hearts, for the coming of the Lord is at hand,* St. James tells us, and the comfort and encouragement of this hope have application to all the trials of a tried Christian life. *Here is the patience of the saints, who keep the commandments of God, and the faith of Jesus.*

22.

The self-denial of a Christian will be for God his Saviour. But this self-denial consists not so much in little matters of food, amusement, employment of time, and other things of like kind, though they are not excluded, as in an entire submission to God in all points of service and duty: in a desire, as all is received from Him, to expend all for Him; to live not as our own masters, but God's servants. Our highest aim should be to serve the will of God, and to say with entire truth, as St. Paul said of himself, *I live, now not I; but Christ liveth in me.* It is the proper character of a true Christian to be able to deny, and as it were, disown himself, and to make a full surrender of self to God; so minding only the will of His Creator, Heavenly King, and Redeemer, as to forget self; and to glory in his own nothingness, and in the fulness of the Godhead, now through the humanity of Christ, his to have communion with and to be filled with. *Of His fulness* (St. John writes) *have we all received, and grace for grace.* This being nothing in himself is the way for the Christian to be all things: this having nothing, the true way to possess all things.

> Lord, at Thy feet I fall,
> I groan to be set free;
> I fain would now obey Thy call,
> And give up all for Thee.
>
> Come and possess me whole;
> Nor hence again remove.
> Settle and fix my wavering soul,
> With all Thy weight of love.

How excellent, then, how much to be cherished, is this Christian self-denial!

23.

Be assured, that we have no need to stay for happiness till we get to Heaven. God is not lovingly present to the ungodly while His omnipotence supports them, and His mercy continues them in being, but he is lovingly present to everyone who is united to Him as His Father in Christ, and imparts Himself to them, according to his creature capacity of reception. And when religion acts on the mind and heart of man, so that he can truly tell to others—*O taste and see the Lord is sweet*; then there is an inward sense of Divine love towards himself, which enables him to say, *thou art the God of my heart, and my portion for ever.* True piety brings in a constant revenue of solid satisfaction to the spirit of the Christian, as he sits by those eternal springs of peace and joy in God which feed and maintain it; while men destitute of religion converse only with the lusts and vanities of this fading life, which buoy them up for a time with unholy joys and a mere shadow of peace, and which passing away, both shadow and substance of happiness are lost eternally to them, the humble, earnest Christian drinks in from the fountain of goodness, and is filled more and more with a peace that passeth understanding till filled with all the fulness of God. Let the consideration of this impress on us God's word by Isaias: *Oh, that thou hadst hearkened to my commandments, thy peace had been as a river, and thy justice as the waves of the sea.*

24.

The advantage of living under the influence of Christian piety is above estimation. It enlarges the heart, according to Holy David's words: *I have run the way of thy Commandments, when thou didst enlarge my heart;* and taking hold of the mind, and of all the faculties of a man, it causes him to reach out to God, and all holy things, without any feeling of confinement or restraint. The nearer any one comes in love and faith to God, who is infinite fulness, the more he finds the truth of the Apostle's word, *where the Spirit of the Lord is there is liberty;* while men without religion and destitute of true godliness, are like shellfish which move up and down imprisoned within what they carry about them. Sin is the sinking of the soul from God, who is desirous to draw it up to Himself, into the slough of sensual selfishness; while Christian piety elevates the soul to God, and causes it to exercise and delight itself in His infinite perfection, as its proper rest and home. A Christian is really most free when under the most powerful and effectual restraint of the fear of God. *If the Son* (Christ said of himself) *shall make you free, you shall be free indeed.* Be sure of this, that if God had not been our supreme and most perfect good, then to have loved Him with all the heart, mind, soul, and strength, would not have been given us, as the *first and greatest commandment.* How grievously then do they err, who, regarding religion as a needful but painful duty, fit their observance of it within as short and scanty measures as they think will satisfy God, and bring them peace at the last. Avoid their error.

23.

From whatever quarter, or cause, evil assails you, let your

first care be employed about yourself. *Be not overcome of evil*, and stand on your defence; but go not unarmed to a certain conflict. *Insinuate humility one to another*, but specially let the breastplate of Christian love sit close on your heart in dealing with other's failings. The time to rebuke is when we love, and this is also and most true, when we contend for our religion, and against its adversaries, or those who molest us on account of it. Endeavour to arm yourself with the same mind that was in Jesus, *who, when he was reviled did not revile; when he suffered, he threatened not*. It may be well to wait till an interval of calm takes place, and then expostulate with your annoyers. There is an unkind and taunting way of speaking to persons who evidently set light by religion and its duties which increases irritation and offence. Spiritual weapons are dangerous when wielded by a hasty hand. *The servant of the Lord must not wrangle, but be mild towards all men, apt to teach, patient; with modesty admonishing them that resist the truth*. You complain of being taunted with your attendance at God's house, and its services, and with the observances and requirements of your Church. Much of the remedy for this is in discovering to such with quiet perseverence, that good will to man, which was so manifested in Christ, when *God sent His Son into the world that we might live through Him*. Your own experience of this blessed truth, this gospel of salvation, will greatly assist you to bring opponents under its guiding and sanctifying influence. Will it not be good to win them over?

26.

We should separate ourselves from reliance on religious feeling as a ground of hope and acceptance with God. This is so important that I press it on your attention. There can be no religion without some religious feeling. It is indispensable to the being a Christian. But there is a disposition in some to trust in their feelings, and to make a kind of idol of them. For instance, you experience, perhaps, at some time, great sorrow for sin, or great thankfulness for mercies, or great lowliness of spirit, or self-humiliation. But if you recall those feelings, and dwell much upon them, and so as to place trust and confidence in them, it will be to your soul's injury. It is not our feelings, but Christ that saves us. Do not be frequently examining and poring over your feelings, past or present. It will lead, most probably, to darkness of mind, dejection of spirit, and perhaps to serious errors. For if you are looking for something in your own feelings, whether of joy or sorrow, or earnestness, or devotion, or what not, on which you place your trust for God's acceptance instead of the all-sufficient and present Saviour and His grace, you are, after all, placing confidence in self, and the result will be to your great spiritual injury. Christ is a jealous Saviour, and will not be undervalued. Religious feelings are valuable only as they unite us more closely to God and Him.

27.

It is almost impossible to speak much, without saying what is injurious, as well as unprofitable. We seem to be under a necessity of sharing to some extent in the train of thought, and experience of others to whom we are speaking, and hardly at liberty to reject subjects pleasing to them. Thus we are led into topics and matters that are far from being religious or edifying. How much (for instance) of ordinary conversation is taken up with remarks on the conduct of and reports about others? How much of suspicion and backsliding is there! To keep clear of this we should acquire the habit of controlling our tongues, and of a conscientious reserve and silence. Besides, how soon by not checking our talkativeness, we get our minds filled with vain and useless thoughts: thus depriving ourselves of the consciousness, so blessed, of the sweet and purifying presence of God. And, as words are outward signs and expressions of inward passions, resentful passions, and anger and contempt of others, will be sure to acquire strength by our unguarded and rash speech. On the contrary, silence will often keep the fire down, till it goes out, deprived of the fuel of words. Remarkable are St. James' words: *If any man offend not in word, the same is a perfect man, able also to lead about the whole body. And the tongue is a fire, a world of iniquity.* Nor less observable is Solomon's proverb: *He that keepeth his mouth, and his tongue, keepeth his soul from distress.* Not a few Christians seem to think that sin attaches more to other parts of conduct than to speech. But let us all remember our Lord's words: *I say unto you that every idle word that men shall speak, they shall render account for it in the Day of Judgment.*

28.

You probably experience, and you will certainly, if you are watchful over yourselves, that there is nothing more unruly than your own self-will. Is it not perpetually hurrying you to and fro by the impulse of various passions; and very specially of pride. It is so where religion does not rule, and it often prevails to rob the true Christian of the enjoyment and blessing of God. It is the seed of the Evil One, at enmity with that heaven-born nature which is the Seed of God in His children. It is the heart of the old Adam within us. And to it may be applied the apostle's words, *I find a law, that when I have a will to do good, evil is present with me.* Where and as it rules, men follow their own fancies and opinions; and make their own boisterous wills, plumb lines to measure the right and wrong of all that comes before them. If a man, instead of submission to, and compliance with, the will of God, sets up his own will, and serves it in his daily life, he exalts himself against God, seeks to live independently of God, and carries on that war against God which as to man Satan began in Eden, and has never ceased to carry on. Now it is the excellency of the Christian religion that it tames the impetuosity and turbulence of our proud self-will. It effects the highest and noblest conquest, when it masters the foe so firmly seated in the centre of our souls. It was the greatest lesson which our dear Lord and Master came to teach us, to deny our own wills. He promoted it by His example, as He says, *I came down from heaven, not to do my own will, but the will of him that sent me.* In his greatest agonies He said, *not my will but thine be done.* So He has taught us to pray, and so to live. Remember that it is the highest dignity conferred upon you, by your Lord and Saviour; and follow after it. Earnestly and prayerfully fight against that spirit of self-will that rises up so proudly against the will of your Father in heaven.

29.

It is said of our Lord by the prophet Malachias: *He is like a refiner's fire, and like the fuller's herb, and he shall sit refining and cleansing the silver.* Nothing more purifies and exalts the soul than religion, when we suffer God to sit within it, *and our members to be the temple of the Holy Ghost who is in us.* The Apostle adds, *glorify, and bear God in your body.* Who can tell the inward life and spiritual vigour that the soul of fallen and sinful man may be filled with, when in conjunction with an Almighty Being? Who can limit that power in the soul which shall discover itself, when the Holy Spirit spreads forth his influences upon it, and its faculties. The more spiritual anything is, the higher, nobler, and more active it is. While all wilful sin wastes and eats out the vigour of the soul, and commences its eternal death, religion awakens and enlivens it, and commences *eternal life.* Therefore he saith, *Rise thou that sleepest, and arise from the dead, and Christ shall enliven thee.* Uniting the soul to God, the centre and source of life and strength, religion produces in a Christian holy courage, calm fortitude, and perseverance unto victory. *They that hope in the Lord shall renew their strength; they shall take wings as eagles; they shall run and not be* weary; *they shall walk and not faint; God* (says St. Paul) *hath not given us the spirit of fear* (sin is this), *but of power.* This is the Christian religion; for does not the same great Apostle say: *I can do all things in Him who strengtheneth me?* Endeavour then to get more and more acquainted with the power of the Gospel salvation, and to rise more under its true influence. While so many around are slaves and captives to one vanity or another, do you seek to prove and give proof to the Church and the world, that you *mind the things above, not the things on the earth; for your life is hid with Christ in God, and when He shall appear you shall appear with him in glory.* Strive thus for the crown that is to be won.

30.

Let me warn you against the indulgence of a spirit of curiosity. It gives the enemy of our souls frequent great advantage to injure us, and to retard us, to say the least, in our progress heavenward. The principle of curiosity, leading us to inquire, obtain information and knowledge, and reflect on what we hear and observe, is good. It attaches to us as rational creatures. It is implanted in men by God. But it often leads us astray, causing us to indulge in much unprofitable reading; in lending an itching ear to political news, and to the circulating gossip of families and of the town we live in. Like the *Athenians* of old, there are some who spend much or most of their daily time (that precious talent given by God to our careful trust and improvement), *in telling or in hearing some new thing.* One of the evils of this spirit of curiosity is, that excluding what is of value, it fills mind and head with what is unprofitable, or worse. The spirit of God will not dwell in a mind pressed down and running over with foolish and vain imaginations, such as the bitterness of party politics, and reports, often idle, often cruel and unjust, of our town and locality. Another evil is that it wars with that *quietness of spirit*, and that *pondering in the heart* of God's words and ways, which marked the character of the Blessed Mother of Our Lord, and is very conducive to our preparation for Eternal Life. Indeed the indulgence of this spirit of curiosity, which so easily possesses us, strikes at the very life of religion in our souls. For the love of news and gossip, become an idol; and has as much power over those who give way to it, as the greed of gold has over a miser. They worship news as much as some worship money. And how can the love of God rule within a heart distracted with passing occurrences, and an unregulated inquiry after reports often untrue, often, if true, not at all concerning us or others to whom we speak of them. Restrain this tendency, and *building yourselves on your most Holy Faith, praying in the Holy Ghost keep yourselves in the love of God, and in patient waiting for Christ.*

31.

What should be the chief end and purpose of our daily life? is a question we do well to put to ourselves, and this is the answer to bring home to our inmost hearts: The glory of God in our recovery to His likeness; or, in other words, our becoming like God. As religion influences and rules in us, we shall be continually returning to Him.

Nothing more confines the mind and heart of any one than the meanness and poverty of the end he is pursuing in his daily life. There is no true liberty to those who are in thraldom to this world, and to some particular interest in it. Low ends and aims debase and degrade us. For we shape ourselves to them, as far as we can. We are turned as *clay to the seal*, as Job says: as Laban's ewes did as to their young, before the watering troughs, so the conception of our minds and hearts take their character from what we keep before them, and if that is earthly only, we become only earthly. But if we make God and His glory our end, and the recovery of His image in our souls our cherished and prized aim, so the more we shall become Godlike, as St. Paul says: *We all, beholding the glory of the Lord with open face, are transformed into the same image, from glory to glory, as by the spirit of the Lord.* See then what a noble and excellent end we all may and should live for. It will be, oh! blessed truth! eternal life begun. How calm and quiet amid all changes, how patient and hopeful under all crosses, how consistent and upright amid all temptations, will the keeping of this end steadily before us make us to be! It will be in some degree the life of everyone that partakes of the Spirit of Christ; as indeed it was His life, to *honour the Father*, the Eternal, Almighty, Infinite Creator, King, and God.

32.

In this is my Father glorified, said Christ, *that you may bring forth very much fruit, and become my Disciples.* Our Lord here teaches us what it is to glorify God, namely, to be fruitful in all holiness, and to live so that our lives may shine with His grace spreading itself through our whole man. But we glorify God rather by receiving the impression of His glory on ourselves than by communicating any glory to Him. We glorify Him best as we become most like Him. We act most for His glory, when a spirit of truth, justice, meekness, kindness, and other graces, pervades our daily conduct. When we so live in the world, as becomes those who converse with that Almighty Being, who made, supports, and governs it, from whom all good flows, and in whom *is no spot, stain, or shadow of evil*; when captivated, as it were, by the sense of His goodness and loveliness, we endeavour to be like Him, and to be conformed, as much as creatures may be, to Him. Our dear Lord did not come into the world to let it see how great and magnificent He was. No; he came, not only to redeem by dying for us, but that we, by participation of the divine nature, and by exercise of divine virtues, such as love, peace, long suffering, kindness, goodness, and truth, should seek to become like Him. There is nothing that one who has any true sense and knowledge of God, can so properly thirst after and seek as participation of the divine nature. We then approve ourselves members of Christ; when our minds and affections are conformed to His, and when He, our Lord and God, approves His sovereignty over all the faculties of our souls, by rendering them as like Himself, as consists with our condition as creatures. This is to answer the end of our Being, our Redemption, and our Calling, and you are invited, and entreated, not to fail of it.

33.

To those of you who have religion at heart, I now more particularly speak; to call your attention to a duty, much neglected, but most becoming a Christian people. This is the asking a blessing and returning thanks at meals. Can it but be most fit, that when we sit down at our tables, we should beg of God to grant His blessing on the food His Providence provides us with? And when we rise, to render Him our thanks for the sustenance we have received? Observe the authority we have in Holy Scriptures for this Christian duty. *Whether ye eat or drink, or whatsoever else you do, do all to the glory of God;* writes St. Paul, after saying, *If I partake with thanksgiving, why am I evil spoken of for that which I give thanks.* Elsewhere he says, *Every creature of God is good, and nothing to be rejected that is received with thanksgiving: for it is sanctified by the word of God and prayer;* and we have the example of our dear Lord and Saviour; *taking the seven loaves and the fishes, and giving thanks, he brake and gave to his disciples. When they were at supper* (we find again) *Jesus took bread, and blessed: and, taking the chalice, he gave thanks:* and, again, *at table with them,* (the two disciples at Emmaus) *he took bread and blessed and brake.* What is called *saying grace,* or *asking a blessing,* was our Lord's custom at meals. Is it so with you? It is often totally neglected; often a mere form, useless, hurried, and irreverent. It becomes you as Christians and Catholics, professing attention to religious duties, not to omit this duty; but to give an example to your neighbours, to observe that in this respect as in others, the resolution of Joshua shall be yours : *As for me and my house, we will serve the Lord.* It may bring on you His blessing, of more value than all this world can give you.

34.

Which is the first commandment with a promise? This : *Honour thy father and thy mother, that it may be well with thee; and thou mayest be long-lived upon the earth.* This, as if St. Paul had said, is a duty of the greatest consequence; distinguished from the other commandments by a special intimation of the favour of God on the observance of it. It is one of the consequences of the particular employment of young people in large manufacturing towns that this great commandment is often sadly disregarded. Obedience, reverence, support, are the duties children owe their parents. I shall confine my remarks to the latter, which includes every kind of assistance that can be given them to render their last days easy and comfortable. It is sad to see old age, which should have only its own infirmities to struggle with, sinking under the pressure of poverty and home discomfort and neglect. The Union is often their refuge, and it is a mercy that such a refuge is provided by the law of the land; and as a general rule, no fault is to be found with the conduct of it. But to keep them from this, and before it is resorted to, and after it is, as may sometimes be best, much may and ought to be done by the sons and daughters to make the closing days of a father or mother's life comfortable and quiet from disturbing cares. There are cheering helps which Christian children should consider it an honour, and happiness as well as a duty, to minister to an aged and feeble parent. These are too often avoided as a burden, not required to be borne by them where there is the Union to take the charge of the aged father or mother, interfering too much with their own occupations, amusements, and indulgences, and so put away altogether. Observe our Lord's strong condemnation of such unnatural behaviour: *God said, Honour thy father and mother.* But you say, *whosoever shall say, the gift whatsoever proceedeth from me shall profit thee, and he shall not honour his father or mother, you have made void the commandment of God.* And what a deep sense of filial duty must our Saviour have had, when in the agonies of death he said to His Blessed mother, *Woman, behold thy son;* and to the disciple, St. John: *Behold thy mother.* God brings neglect of this commandment as a heavy charge against the Jews. Keep this in mind, and lay it to heart, and prove that you do so by your filial kindness.

35.

Judge not, (said our Lord), *that ye be not judged.* Our religious state is very defective, when we are ready to pronounce judgment on others, yet avoid to judge ourselves. The first is seldom our duty; the latter always is. It is a good rule, when we observe a fault in another, to see if we may not find two, perhaps greater, faults in ourselves. To suspect is not to judge, but is a step towards it; and, therefore, as a general rule, be not suspicious of evil. The habit of suspecting and judging others, marks that defect of character which we find in indolent persons, who take little heed of their own words or actions, while very ready to pick to pieces those of others. An old writer says, " it is a property of those who are diligent in judging and condemning others, to be very negligent as to their own faults." Thus the Jews (St. Paul writes) judged the heathens, themselves being quite as evil, or worse, in life. Let us then, from this day forward, be careful to observe and judge ourselves, and let our prayer be, *" Enter not into judgment with thy servant, O Lord, for in thy sight shall no man living be justified,* for the necessity of this petition will be a sure result of close and honest self-observance.

36.

By one man, sin entered into the world, and death by sin. Thus says Holy Scripture, and the record of every human being reads us the same awful and humbling fact. There are two threads which tie together the whole race of mankind; man's sin and God's mercy, which, through Christ, becomes to all who receive it, salvation to eternal life. No one who reads his Bible carefully can shut his eyes to the statements which meet him in it, of the reality, extent, guilt, and danger of sin. Blessed are they who seeing this in the light of Christ, of his Gospel, and his Church, fix the eye of their souls on Him who came into our world, and died on the cross that we might live through Him. Such can say, *I thank my God, through Jesus Christ, my Lord.* Such can lay hold of the promise, *There is now no con-*

demnation to them that are in Christ Jesus, who walk not according to the flesh. The law of the spirit of life in Christ Jesus delivers them from the law of sin and death. Far more quickening to the soul than the vital heat of the prophet Elisha to the dead body of the Shunamite's child, is the grace of the Holy Spirit. Let our constant prayer be

> Come, Holy Ghost, Creator come,
> From Thy bright heavenly throne;
> Come, take possession of our souls,
> And make them all Thy own.

37.

Nothing, but the life of God in the soul, can properly be called life. They who go astray from God, His will and commandments, are *dead*. Hence St. Paul says, *You hath He quickened, who were dead in trespasses and sins.* The life of God communicated in holy baptism, ceases in those who live in wilful sin; and they must be recreated and born again, to have God restored to dwell in them. The death of Christ is not enough, nor is it all we need for our salvation. Unless there is a restoration within us of the image of God, we are not only, not in a state of readiness to dwell with Him, but in a state of alienation from Him. What importance this gives to earnestness in all religious duties, to prayer and watchfulness! to take heed *not to grieve the Holy Spirit of God, whereby we are sealed unto the day of redemption.* What a different thing does this show the Christian life to be, from a mere keeping up of forms and ceremonies, or mere customary regard to the external requirements of the Church. We must have, and seek to maintain the life of God in our own daily lives. The apostle means this, when he says: *To me, to live is Christ.* May God help us to understand and act on this!

38.

It is observable that only four female ancestors of our Lord Jesus Christ, according to the flesh, are named in the Gospels. Of these four, three are marked in Holy Scripture, by some great immorality, and three were of Heathen descent, and not of God's Israel. By this fact we may consider our Blessed Lord and Saviour as foreshowing His merciful kindness towards sinners, and that the Gentiles as well as the Jews, should share in the benefit of His incarnation and death, and be enlightened with the light of His Salvation. This blessed truth is indeed patent throughout Holy Scripture. But we learn further that the sins of parents bring no true dishonour on their pious children, and that when any one lives as a Christian should live, we ought not to recall to mind what his parents may have been, except to admire the Grace of God towards and in the son or daughter. Let us also remember that *each one will have to give account of himself to God;* and that as in the case of these four female ancestors of Christ, so often now, *where sin hath abounded, grace doth much more abound.*

39.

One great point of prudence requisite in an earnest Christian is not to overtax his bodily strength with excessive work, nor his mind by too much care about worldly business. And there certainly should be a like and equal discretion in spiritual duties. Excess may choak devotion; and a care for the salvation of others (it will be well, for all who minister to others in holy things, to have in mind) cause a neglect of our own. That truly saintly man, the Marquis de Renty, gives this wise advice in a letter to a friend: " Give me leave to deal plainly with you, in telling you, that among the many cares I have for you, this is not the least, that you do not lay too much on yourself, and for want of moderation in the service of Christ and His Church, render yourself altogether unserviceable. The enemy of the Saviour, of the Church, and people, takes no small advantage of *such indiscretion.* A Christian is not his own, but with St. Paul, *a debtor,* in his degree, *to all men.* Preserve yourself, therefore, not so much by making much of yourself, as by forbearing to weaken and destroy yourself, by excess in devotion, fastings, and labours for others." This is not now a frequent mistake, far from it; but there are some of you, and in every large congregation, to whom the caution may be of use, especially in Lent.

40.

Our temptations, through the artifices of our Satanic enemy, are often adapted to bring out feelings and desires, which are wrong in their very nature, and, therefore, ought not to have acceptance with us at all. Our Saviour was tempted, by having the kingdoms and wealth of the world put before him, with the view of his desiring them, for his personal enjoyment and aggrandisement. The temptation went no further than the intellectual perception or apprehension. It had no effect on his desires or will. It secured no pleased or consentient action on his part, but was instantly rejected. The same may be said of the temptation to throw himself down from the Temple. With respect to the intellect, it was doubtless understood; or otherwise, it could hardly be regarded as a temptation. But it found no entrance into the heart. With regard to ourselves, this may be called an innocent stage of temptations. They must exist intellectually, and be perceived and thought of, or there could hardly be such a thing as temptation. But they may exist to this extent, and be perceived and felt by us, to exist, without sin. Neither the desires nor affections, nor the conscience, or the will are asleep or insensible, but are awake and sensible of the danger, and at once repel the assault. Keeping this in mind, *Resist the Devil and he will fly from you.*

41.

It is part of Christian duty to endeavour to understand the nature of temptations. I would have you therefore to keep in mind that a temptation may go beyond the apprehension of the intellect, and take effect in the emotions and desires, and yet there may be no sin. For there are emotions and desires quite right and lawful in their nature, and only wrong in their degree or circumstances. The object which in this case tempts is presented to our intellect, and thence received into the affections, and taken pleasure in, in some measure or degree. The desire to take food or drink is natural and right. The temptation to seek it may pass from the intellect to the heart, so as to excite the desire for it, but if it does not pass the due limit, there is no sin. *In David's longing for the water of the cistern of Bethlehem* there was no sin; and he kept it within limit when he would not drink of it, because his friends *brought it to him with the danger of their lives*, but *offered it to the Lord.* This limit, both as circumstances and degrees, varies greatly, and depends much on our position and responsibilities. In persons who *watch unto prayer*, there will be ever a conscious perception of danger, when a temptation passes that boundary in our natural desires which it ought not to pass. So long as this is heeded, and the temptation to go beyond it is repelled, there is no sin. This may be a relief to some scrupulous minds, and encourage others to persevere in the path of godliness.

42.

It may be well worth your attention, and to keep in mind, that the temptations of a Christian will often be violent in proportion to the resistance made by him to them. It may seem, but is, no contradiction, that the holier any one is, the more violent will be the temptations which at times he has to endure. A person who yields to temptations frequently, in whole or in part, will not understand their full force. Satan has no inducement to exert his strength against the man who yields easily. But he who is resolute, with the help of his Saviour, not to sin at all; who would die rather than commit wilful or mortal sin; who opposes the whole energy of his renewed nature, of *the new man in Christ Jesus*, to the assaults of the Evil One, will experience the power and craft of the enemy that wages war against him. Satan hates true godliness, and whatever is included in it. He hates it in general and in particular; and whoever proposes, in aiming to lead a godly and Christian life, to serve God in some particular duty, or to do better in some particular course of action, will find it true of the Evil One, and his temptations, as our Lord said of His Apostles, *Satan hath desired to have you, that he may sift you as wheat.* But take comfort and courage from our Lord's added words, true to every earnest and faithful Christian: *I have prayed for thee that thy faith fail not.* Have faith in Christ, and Satan will be baffled.

43.

Let me add some further remarks on the subject of temptations. Endeavour to remain re-collected, and in a spirit of patience, when the temptation is upon you. *In your patience you shall possess your souls.* The Devil gains advantage, if he can disturb our peace. Your heavenly Father is present with you, permitting the temptation for His own glory, and your spiritual good, and He will not let it go further than He sees needful for these great objects. Let the recollection of this exclude disquieting thoughts. Exercise faith in your Lord and Saviour, for truly this is the great secret of a Christian power. St. Paul found it so, when suffering from the *sting in the flesh*, or the *messenger of Satan*; so that he says: *When I am weak, then I am powerful;* and St. Jude speaks of God as *able to preserve us without sin.* Having learned to live by faith, which to many is a new, and to very many it must be feared a hidden way of life, the prayer of a true Christian goes up to the Throne of God rapidly, so as to meet and confront the temptation as soon as it is presented to the mind. The prayer of a true and living faith is a mighty prayer: it has power with the Omnipotent God: it touches the heart of Infinite Love: it brings upon the soul the shield and covering of a present Redeemer and Sanctifier, the Godman Jesus Christ. Temptation is a profitable trial of the Christian life, suited to purify and strengthen the work of grace in us: *seeming not to bring with it joy, but sorrow, but afterwards yielding to them who are exercised by it the most peaceful fruits of justice.* Our dear Lord *learned obedience by the things which he suffered; and He suffered, being tempted.* Be content thus to bear His cross.

44.

Jerusalem (says the Holy Psalmist) *is built as a city which is compact together.* This has a true application to the upright and faithful Christian, and in proportion as he corresponds with the work of divine grace in his soul. For that grace more and more reduces all the faculties of the soul into subjection to itself. God, as known in and through Christ, is a being so holy, so good, so lovely, so attractive, so adequate to the largest capacities of the highest creature, that where His grace is truly operative, it unites to Himself the whole renewed man. *The old things are passed away: all things are made new.* The entire life becomes under the sweet rule of supreme goodness. This is the true rest of our souls, when all our faculties with their various exercises and movements, meet like so many lines in one and the same centre, God. If there were not this centre, and if the fallen creature, man, could not return to it, he would be a most wretched and distracted being. There could be no true abiding satisfaction for him : but the words of Isaias would have their application to him, as they have to all without religion : *Why do ye spend money for that which is not bread, and your labour for that which doth not satisfy you? Incline your ear and come to me* (says God), *hear and your soul shall live.* When the knowledge of God or Christ enters into the soul and possesses it, it subdues its self-will, lulls its sinful and worldly appetites, and shewing to it the fountain of supreme goodness and happiness, gives it in *drawing water out of the wells of salvation,* a *peace that passeth understanding* ; a *joy unspeakable and full of glory,* a true contentment in an experienced recovery of the divine image, which is the great design of God in our redemption and calling.

48.

There is a measure of religious experience, which may properly be termed the life of God in any one who becoming conscious of his guilt and sinfulness, and seeking heartily and honestly to Christ as a Saviour, enters, however feebly, on a new life. This life, though different in its character from that of the world around, and such as in due time, if the means of grace are carefully used, will expand itself into heights and depths of spiritual existence, is still only incipient as the life of God. It is only as the early dawning of a brighter and fuller day. There is a higher, more advanced, and confirmed spiritual state of a Christian, a life in intimate union with God, which may be fitly called the interior life, and should be the aim and pursuit of every one. To this the Psalmist may refer, when he says: *As the hart panteth after the fountains of waters, so my soul panteth after thee, O God.* And St Paul: *I live, now not I, but Christ liveth in me.* And when he writes to the Colossians: *If you be risen with Christ seek the things that are above—for you are dead, and your life is hid with Christ in God.* And the Saviour seems to refer to this interior and higher and true spiritual life in the Apocalypse: *To him that overcometh will I give the hidden manna, and a white counter, and in the counter a new name written, which no man knoweth, but he that receiveth it.* This interior life is peculiarly the life of those, who progressing beyond the first elements of Christianity, are seeking truly to be *sanctified in Christ Jesus; and to go on to things more perfect.* There is in them the living principle of eternal life, so fixed, and a *renewing unto knowledge, according to the image of them that created them,* such as no other form of Christian life can compare with it in the fruits and results. Indeed, let the world deride, and many called Christians despise and neglect it, yet this is that life of God, which will well repay (what is our proper Christian calling) its diligent, immediate pursuit, *And this we pray for, your perfection.*

46.

Observe carefully, that the interior life, which a Christian should cultivate, as the preparation for, and earnest of eternal life, is the result of union with Christ. *Because I live* (said the Lord) *and you shall live.* Also, *I am the vine* (He said again), *you are the branches. He that abideth in me, and I in him, the same beareth much fruit, for without me ye can do nothing.* He, whose *life is hid with Christ in God,* will not doubt that His spiritual growth is sustained only in that divine source. It is a life the world neither knows nor appreciates. *The world knoweth not us,* (writes St. John) *because it knew not Him.* A man of the world understands and appreciates a man of the world, and many who profess to be Christians have such a mixture of the world and of religion in their principles of action and daily life, that men of the world can pretty well understand. and appreciate them. But of the interior life of that Christian who truly follows after holiness of heart and life, and loves it for its own sake, they have no clear idea. They are quite at a loss to understand the intimacy and friendship which there is between God and the sanctified heart and mind. They who in the principles of their lives are saints, can alone understand, so as to properly appreciate, saints. Herein in part is the communion of saints. *The sensual man perceiveth not these things that are of the Spirit of God; for it is foolishness to him, and he cannot understand, because it is spiritually examined. But the spiritual man judgeth all things, and himself is judged of no man.* See, to what an high pursuit you are called: follow after it, that you may attain. Give God an whole heart. Why will ye be *unwise and hate knowledge*, when God says, *I will utter my spirit to you, and shew you my words?* and when *the spirit searcheth all things*; *yea, the deep things of God*, and shews them to the sons of God.

47.

That interior life to which God calls you is very different from the life of the world. Men under the influence of worldly principles seek notoriety, even in their Christian profession. They love *to be called Rabbi*. Even in their religious duties they desire to *be seen in the market place, and at the corners of the streets.* But where the soul is really occupied with a divine companionship, there will be no desire to see, or to be seen openly, except when and where duty calls. There will be willingness to be little, unhonoured, and even cast out from among men. There will be no eye for worldly pomp, nor ready ear for popular applause. The Divine Saviour, the highest personage the world ever saw, or will see in it, when He came into it, on the highest errand, was so humble in origin, so simple in appearance, so gentle in heart and manner, that the world could not comprehend Him: He was as a sealed book, but all who are under the influence of the interior and truly spiritual life have the key to open it with. Therefore, St. Paul writes, *Let this mind be in you which was also in Christ Jesus, who emptied Himself, taking the form of a servant.* Many care not for anything in religion but its externals, but there ever have been, and still are, *sons and daughters of the Most High* on whose regenerated hearts Christ writes His name, and from whose inmost souls the Holy Spirit raises up an incense of loving service, which goes up silently to Heaven, but of which St. Paul's words are true: *We are the good odour of Christ unto God.* Cultivate this, for it is the true Christian life. It is the real fragrance of the profession of religion.

48.

It was a sin of the Pharisees that *they loved the glory of men more than the glory of God,* and the Lord reproached them with it: *How can you believe, who receive glory one from another, and the glory which is from God alone you do not seek?* Oh, that we may rise above this earthly worldly propensity, and become dead to this fatal principle which detains thousands, in the heartless mummeries of an heartless world, and checks the aspirations of even pious minds. Why did St. Paul from a pupil of Gamaliel become a servant of Christ? Because he became dead to this feeling of worldly estimation, and no longer sought to *please men, but God,* and *condescended not to flesh and blood.* Why did he *withstand St. Peter to the face, because he was to be blamed?* Because, as he says, *with me it is a very small thing to be judged by you, or by man's day; he that judgeth me, is the Lord.* Whence shall we gain the true nobility of Christian feeling and character, or make progress in the Christian life; but only so far as we are dead to regard to worldly estimation, so that we may live to Christ: only as we renounce meaner springs of action, and live on that principle of a renewed mind, to *live the rest of his time in the flesh, not after the desires of man, but according to the will of God.* So, do you also reckon that you are dead to sin, but alive unto God, through Christ Jesus our Lord. Live, *not as pleasing men, but God who proveth our hearts.*

49.

Our feelings towards others will be very much as our feelings within ourselves; and our feelings within ourselves will be, according to our faith in God, through Christ. Hence, as we have faith in God, so will be our kindness towards men. So true it is that *Faith worketh by love.* And this: *Every one that loveth is born of God, and knoweth God.* And this also: *In this we know that we love the children of God, when we love God, and keep His commandments.* The peace which dwells within us will seek for objects over which to shed its own calm and blessedness. It will press outwards therefore towards our fellow men; softening what is evil in them; believing with the hope of charity all that should be found in them; bearing with meek patience all that is aggressive in them; dispersing abroad, with free and cheerful liberality, all that may be useful to them; obscuring and chastening down to the view all that is harsh, angular, and repugnant in them, as the brilliant haze of a fine October day softens down the hard outlines of a landscape, and mellows each object into a broad neutral tint of mild splendour. Do you desire to possess or increase in yourselves this most valuable and blessed state of heart and mind? Go to God, and He will give it you; wait on Him, and He will cause it to grow within you. Let your prayer be: *Lord, increase our faith*, and the result will be that the same Holy Spirit, by which Jesus answered their prayer, who then made it, will answer yours. You will exemplify St. Peter's advice: *Purifying your souls in the obedience of charity, with a brotherly love; from a sincere heart, love one another earnestly.* This is true Catholicity, and the spirit of the Catholic Church in her well instructed individual members.

50.

Consider well and lay to heart the record we have of the affection of an eminent French ecclesiastic (lately deceased) for the Holy Scripture. The word of God was always on his table. He kissed its pages with respect, read a few verses, and stopped at each thought that struck him, desirous to meditate and penetrate the spiritual sense. Towards the end of his life he said: "I have read this book for thirty years, and every day I discover in it new lights and new depths. How different it is from the word of man! That is exhausted at a single draught, but the word of God is a bottomless abyss!" How much (he wrote) are unbelievers to be pitied as they advance in life! The light becomes so lively, so sweet, so penetrating in proportion as we draw near to death under the auspices of faith, and of virtue, which has its root in the gospel. We no longer believe only. We see. In the same way as the mystery of iniquity increases in an unbelieving soul, and everything becomes to him a puzzle and object of doubt, so the light extends and envelopes a soul accustomed to live in God. When I read the gospel, every word seems to me as a flash of lightning, and gives me new consolation." The gospels were in fact his favorite study, and in the New Testament his preference was for St. John and St. Paul, the Apostle of Love, and the Doctor of the Cross. The epistles of St. Paul, which (he says) "I read every day, enchant me more and more with the truth. They are an ocean of which God alone is the shore." Is not this an instruction and a reproof for many of you? Of some who have not I fear a copy of the Holy Scriptures, or of the New Testament, so easily and cheaply obtained? Of some who let day after day pass without looking into it, or treasuring up a single text to be (St. Francis of Sales observes) " as a sweet flower to smell to," amid your daily cares and occupations?

51.

The day being thus begun, as St. Francis of Sales advises, in union with God, and in the meditation of His word, that eminent servant of Christ, whose testimony to the value of Holy Scripture has been on a former morning brought to your notice, found no difficulty in preserving the perfume of his first thoughts by the exercise of recollection, and the remaining hours flowed on peacefully and devoutly. Thus he *walked with God.* His pure and upright soul sought Him alone, and found Him without difficulty. His divine providence, amid the thousand accidents of his life, seemed to lead him on as by the hand. It was his favourite habit often to raise his heart to God, in order to offer to Him his actions, his sufferings, and his work. "I abandon myself to God (he said), and His goodness fills me more and more with gratitude and adoration. I frequently feel my heart spring up towards Him; though it is hardly possible for me to follow any regular course of meditation; the love of the Holy Scriptures increases in me, and I seem to comprehend their sense better than I ever did before." Is there not here something worthy of our endeavour of resemblance? Then let us set about it, and let us taste and see how good the Lord is. Let us (as he did) see and recognize God our Father in Heaven, in all events of life, whether sad or joyous. We shall find, as the Holy Psalmist says again and again, that *God is our strong refuge*, and that in Him *His children have a place of refuge*. None who truly seek God are disappointed. Their mind is

> My God and Father while I stray,
> Far from my home, on life's rough way;
> Oh teach me from my heart to say,
>   Thy will be done.
>
> Let but my fainting heart be blest,
> With Thy sweet spirit for its guest,
> My God to Thee, I leave the rest,
>   Thy will be done.

52.

You all know enough about Judas Iscariot, to concur in Christ's awful words respecting him: *It were better for him if that man had not been born*. I will call your thoughts to him now, to show the end to which association in sin may conduct. Sin began on earth by severing the bond between man and his Maker, and what bond between man and man can henceforth be regarded as permanent? Sin, if left to work its will, would separate God's intelligent creatures into atoms of selfishness. It is observable that while the cross of Christ was being raised as a centre of spiritual attraction, and of union of man with man, sin exhibited its opposite character of selfish repulsion in its darkest colours, in the case of Judas. Sin produces, as in him, a separation of heart from the good and the pious, with whom we may be mixing in common life, and in the House of God. If this is felt, as often it is, by the touches of conscience, delay not repentance and change of life. Break off the bond of besetting sin, and of evil companions, at once and resolutely. Companionship with the good and pious, when it is only formal, customary, and really hypocritical, will not please God, nor benefit ourselves. It is a tie that may be broken at any time, as was the case of Judas and the eleven Apostles, with whom he had been joined. David's prayer, *Let my heart be undefiled in thy justifications, that I may not be confounded*, was reversed in Judas's case. Sin is like a combustible material, which if it once explodes may leave the soul a shattered and hopeless wreck: and whatever strips sin of its true deformity, and gives it to you in a milder and attractive character, and all temporising and coquetting with it, whether it be in your own heart, or in association with others, is full of this danger; till, like the play of children with lucifers, it fires, to what may be an irreparable ruin. *Blessed is the man who hath not walked in the council of the ungodly, nor stood in the way of sinners.*

53.

Learn another lesson from the case of Judas Iscariot. Do not think that sin in the heart is quite the same as when thrown into some outward act. They are in the same line, as Holy Scripture teaches, but the outward act gives sin a power it had not before. When Judas had become the betrayer of his master, he began to realize what he had done and what he had lost. He felt that he had no longer part nor lot with the eleven faithful disciples. The outward act of sin is commonly only the discovery of the previous secret corruption of heart and life. This is God's way of showing men now what the day of judgment will fully open out, that the wicked can no more have fellowship with those, nor a portion, where and with whom they never had any true share. It will be as it is written: *the wicked shall not rise again in judgment, nor sinners in the council of the just.* In this terrible isolation Judas turned to his accomplices. He could not expect that these would relax their hold of Christ, for his confession of evil done by him. But here the gulph of separation opens out again. *What is that to us,* told him that as he had cut himself off from the holy and good, he was cast off by the wicked. Ah! there is no fearful pit of solitude and darkness like that which we may make for ourselves by sin. It has this curse upon it, that it divides us from those whose friendship is worth having, and forms no tie with others that will endure. *My son* (does it not say to us), *if sinners shall entice thee consent thou not. Have no fellowship with the unfruitful works of darkness,* either in heart or life.

54.

One more lesson from the traitor Judas, may be usefully noted by you. When a man cannot endure to be alone with his own thoughts, he may be said to be deserted by himself. This is another consequence of sin and of evil association. There is a very terrible self desertion when conscience is aroused, and a man's own thoughts become intolerable from the sense of his own evil, and when his conscience does within the work of the handwriting on Belshazzar's palace wall. It may be seldom in this world that any one is brought to such blackness of darkness; but every sin a man consciously commits makes him less capable to keep company with himself. All association with evil tends to the coming on of the result of making him who gives in to it try to escape from his own thoughts. And after this association has made man so that he cannot bear to look steadily into his own soul, then his enjoyment of that for which he has sold all that was real, good, and divine, has passed away. He is as a field over which a totally destructive blight, killing all, once fair, verdant, promising, has passed. It was so with Judas. Having denied his master, forsaken his godly companions, despised and rejected by his ungodly tempters, and unable to bear the reproaches of his own conscience, *casting down the pieces of silver in the temple, he went and hanged himself.* Men can put evil friendships and many worldly occupations in God's room so as to forget Him. But when they pass, as pass they must, and the soul is compelled to look on eternal realities, then will be felt that of which the Saviour speaks: *What exchange shall a man give for his soul?* Never then give place to any thing that will cloud your clear filial view of God, weaken your humble yet firm trust in Christ, or grieve that Holy Spirit for the loss of whose dwelling in you there is no conceivable equivalent. Grieve not the Holy Spirit of God, whereby you are sealed unto *the day of redemption. Watch and pray that ye enter not into temptation.*

55.

It is commonly in the conduct and the life that those departures from the narrow way of godliness occur, by which souls that once seemed to bid fair for heaven are lost. The enemy finds it easier to inject actual impurity into the life of a Catholic than error into his belief. A shaken faith will lead the life astray, but a life going astray will often make a total shipwreck of the faith. Departure from godliness and purity in actual life is a mainstay of Satan's kingdom. A successful assault by that enemy on either side endangers all, but in the battle of life and work, conduct is more exposed to danger than profession. While erroneous doctrines are, like Saul, destroying their thousands, indulged lusts, like David, slay their ten thousands. Would that young men and women, in the place and hour of temptation, and in all large towns both are met with daily, might call to mind the apostle's words: *Dearly beloved, I beseech you as strangers and pilgrims to refrain yourselves from carnal desires, which war against the soul.* We are all travelling across time, toward eternity, and we have each, in his custody, the most precious of created things; his own soul. You may lose it, and you certainly endanger it, if you turn aside out of the narrow way of a godly and a Christian life. Stray not from the path, for the treasure you carry is of incalculably more value than any which the Australian diggers carry; who keep the known and proper road and the daylight, march in company, and close by the guard sent to protect them, for the country is wild, and robbers are around. *My son* (God says), *keep my commandments, and thou shalt live, and my law as the apple of thy eye*. The world is evil, and profligate men and women are everywhere around. Keep in Christ's Holy Catholic Church. Persevere in the way of watchful self-danger, and godly living, lest you lose your soul in the end, and mourn when the loss is irreparable.

36.

Anger, except when it is an holy emotion directed against an unholy thing, is a cause of both sin and suffering, and unless we have attained considerably to the wisdom and stature of perfect men in Christ, we can seldom take this fire of anger in our bosom without burning thereby ourselves or our neighbours. Let anyone who tries to crucify the flesh, and to please God, look into his own experience, and he will find that the less he has felt of anger the better it has been for the peace of his conscience and the usefulness of his life. The holy may use anger against sin in the world, but it is too sharp a weapon for the handling of most of us, even in this case. The best practical treatment of anger against others is to defer it. A wise man, though he experiences the heat, will do nothing till he cools again. He will thus both follow the safe course, and be in a better state to form a righteous judgment as to what offends him. But the best specific against anger, either as a sin or a suffering, is *looking unto Jesus*. Its dangerous and tormenting flame, when kindled in our hearts, may best be extinguished by letting in upon it a measure of *that charity wherewith he loved us*. Let us call to mind His own most precious prayer : *I have made known to them Thy name, and will make it known, that the love wherewith Thou has loved me, may be in them, and I in them*. If we abide in Him sinful anger will be kept down or cast out, and what remains, being like His own, will neither trouble ourselves, nor hurt others.

57.

Let me now call your attention to the apostle's words, *Redeeming the time*. There is no bringing back yesterday ; and all time once gone is gone for ever. *Redeeming the time* is then improving present opportunities, and (as the words refer especially to Christians) *to grow in grace and in the knowledge of our Lord and Saviour Jesus Christ*. Every situation of life has its opportunities and its advantages for this redemption of time ; for it brings with it trials of our faith, our patience, our submission to God's will, our affection to, and preference of our Saviour and His grace in ourselves and others, above all present and passing attractions and engagements. And our *redeeming the time*, in the highest sense, consists in using these opportunities, and turning them to advantage in being thus *wise unto salvation*. Do not suppose that if you were in this or that position you could better carry out the apostle's exhortation. Every situation has its temptations, its difficulties, and its advantages, and if you have God with you, you may in it *grow in grace*. Meet seriously, and submissively, and prayerfully, whatever is before you; and instead of turning from the daily duty and the daily conflict, *put on the armour* God has provided, *fight the good fight of faith, and lay hold on eternal life*. If you thus redeem the time, you will hear at last the joyful words: *Because thou hast been faithful over a few things, I will place thee over many things; enter thou into the joy of thy Lord*.

58.

The holy Psalmist says, *Thy comforts have given joy to my soul*. Can we say so? Of all the comforts any one has, the best are internal, and lying in the thoughts and dispositions of the heart; for those are our greatest, truest comforts with which God is pleased, and when there are thoughts and dispositions of which He is the source and subject, they please Him, and will give us true joy. God makes our truest comforts lie at home; in the exercise of our highest faculties, and as it were in secret. *The heart that knoweth the bitterness of his own soul, in his joy the stranger shall not intermeddle*. If we are under the right influence of godly wisdom, whether we are walking, sitting, or lying down, whether we are rich or poor, our coats coarse or fine, our dwellings large and well furnished, or mean and small, God gives us that to think upon, and cherish within, that will *give joy to our souls.* What can make a man miserable that can think thus well, and be so wisely disposed? Nothing will; nobody can. He may have intervening cares, and meet with buffetings of trials. The comforts of God will not shut out all anxious thoughts. They did not from some of the greatest saints of Scripture, as Abraham, David, Elijah, and St. Paul. But if Divine comforts are understood and enjoyed by us there is not one temptation or trial, that we shall not surmount, or that shall separate us from Him. Bless God then for having brought near to you such a subject for your thoughts as Jesus Christ and His great salvation, such an object of the most elevating and holy dispositions. Dwell and meditate upon it, and you will find in your experience that as Nehemiah said, *the joy of the Lord is our strength.*

59.

The Prophet Malachias foretells of Christ, *He shall purify the sons of Levi, and shall refine them as gold and silver.* Though specially applicable to the clergy, it is not without application to all the faithful, who, St. Peter reminds them, *as living stones are built up to offer up spiritual sacrifices acceptable to God by Jesus Christ.* The power for this, *your reasonable service,* as St. Paul called it, is of God, the Holy Ghost, but its experience in ourselves must be found in a diligent use of the Sacraments and all the means of grace. Be frequent in consideration of this your calling; meditate often and with seriousness on this your proper duty, character, and privilege. Be frequent and devout readers of Holy Scripture. Strive to enter into the spirit of the Holy Psalmist, in his estimation of those Scriptures, and often call to mind your Lord's prayer to His Father, for his Disciples: *Sanctify them in truth. Thy word is truth.* Remember, too, St. Paul's commendation of Holy Scripture to Timothy, as that *which can instruct thee to salvation, by the faith which is in Christ Jesus.* And stamp your reading and meditation of Holy Scripture on your understandings and hearts, so that they may be exhibited in your dispositions, words, and actions, by adding persevering, earnest prayer. Thus keep alive the spark that inflames you; thus cherish the grace of God within you; thus turn His word into power and life. In this reading of Holy Scripture and prayer, the Lord will work in your souls as a *refiner of gold and silver.* He will *purge out the dross* of sin, and present you now in His Church on earth, and hereafter in His Heavenly Temple, an offering to His Father in justice and holiness. This is what Christ wants of us all. Woe unto us if we fail to answer this most merciful and glorious design!

60.

Avoid, as you would a venomous serpent, the error of supposing that you may wilfully sin and not suffer for it in consequence. Beware of being influenced by others to act on this supposition. For this will be to put aside the whole testimony of God's word, a great mass of recorded and traditional facts, and what is weightier, it will contradict and condemn the teaching of the cross of Christ. You put the crucified Saviour to an open shame, not only by the sin you presumptuously commit, but in thus declaring that in suffering *the just for the unjust,* He suffered without adequate cause. For God did not overlook or pass by sin in Him who *was wounded for our iniquities,* and *bruised for our sins.* Will He, can you presume to think, pass it by in us, when we wilfully commit iniquity? You perhaps think of your sin, "It is a little one." But can any wilful violation of God's known will and commandments be little? The Psalmist says: *Who can understand sins? From my secret ones cleanse me, O Lord.* How much more, surely, from known and presumptuous sins? We read again: *Wherefore hath the wicked provoked God? He hath said in his heart, he will not require it.* But, *Thou seest it,* the Psalmist says. Keep yourself, then, from the suffering you must have in time or eternity, as that which as surely follows wilful sin, as a consequence can follow an adequate cause in due time; and when conscience brings it home to you, be quick to repent thoroughly, to confess, and to seek pardon. Delay not, but hasten to Jesus, having this encouragement: *My little children* (writes St. John), *these things I write to you that you may not sin. But if any man sin, we have an Advocate with the Father, Jesus Christ the Just,* and *He is the propitiation for our sins.*

61.

Jesus Christ, revealed to the soul by faith, in the use of the Sacraments, in the reading of Holy Scripture, by meditation and prayer, is the true principle of spiritual life. We live to God by going out of ourselves; and we become not only servants of Christ, but partakers of, by thus looking unto Him. As by the telescope we draw a distant object towards us, till it fills our sphere of vision, and we seem translated from the spot we stand on to what we thus behold, so our spiritual life passes out of itself into the higher Being; to what our faith in the use of the various means of grace draws us to, and draws Him to us. As some lower creatures, it is said, change their colour according to the food they feed on, so are we transformed by what we receive within us as the daily food of our soul's spiritual communion. The realities on which we learn to live become our real life. We know not what we are advancing to hereafter, but we may know that we here dwell in Christ, and Christ in us; are one with Christ and Christ with us. And then we receive the full consolation of what St. John writes, *dearly beloved, we are now the son of God, and it hath not yet appeared what we shall be; we know that when He shall appear we shall be like Him, because we shall see Him as He is. Every one that hath this hope in Him, sanctifieth himself, even as He also is holy.* Keep these things in mind, and they will not be advice thrown away.

62.

The incense which the Church appoints to be offered at her altars at her holy services is attractive in its fragrancy, and edifying in its Scriptural significance, to the devout worshipper; but there is no incense more sweet, and more acceptable to God, than our loving confidence in Him. A Christian who finds himself in the great mercy of God, partaker of the divine nature, and transforming through the sanctifying grace of the Holy Ghost into the divine image, takes a real delight in God his Saviour, and in communion with Him. He can say of Christ, *He is my beloved, and my friend*, and with David, *I will take delight in the Lord.* St. John gives us the fullest description of Him, when he tells us *God is charity, and he that abideth in charity abideth in God and God in him.* Is not this a blessed state, when any one, reposing trustfully in Him, in whom he finds only love and loveliness, puts forth his most precious affections of love, confidence, and joy; he gets above fears, and despondencies, and is in a bright, clear region of peaceful, hopeful rest. There is, be assured, an inward sense in the soul of man which if once mastered and excited with an inward taste and relish of God, would better define God than all teachings from men or books. A true Christian—watchful, prayerful, humble, earnest Christian—tastes and sees how good and sweet God is, as none else does. *The God of hope fills him with joy and peace in believing, so that he abounds in hope.* He reposes in God, *his heart is strengthened, he shall not be moved, until he look over his enemies.* Is not this a state to be sought by us? Let us not be so satisfied as we are to go on in a cold formality, like an artistically shaped thurible, without the fire and incense. While the children of the world, like shell fish on the sands left by the receding tide, gape after their accustomed element, and die away deprived of its pleasures and pursuits, true Christians may realise Christ's words,

Whosoever drinketh of the water that I shall give him shall never thirst, but it shall be in him a well of water, springing up into everlasting life.

63.

The truths of our holy religion are not to be trifled with. *They are an odour of life unto life, or of death unto death.* It is to be feared that not a few listen to pious instructions, and sound improvements of the Gospel of Christ, who go away from church not only without any love to God and His truths, but to renew a life of disobedience to His commandments, and to form and execute even guilty purposes. As the Pharisees, after hearing Jesus, and his life-giving words, went away to take council against Him, so it is with some now, who keep up a profession of the Catholic faith. What a proof this is of the evil and deceitfulness of the heart of man! Well might David say: *To day if ye shall hear his voice, harden not your hearts;* and how seasonable is our Lord's warning: *Take heed how ye hear.* The advice of the wise man is very applicable: *Keep thy foot when thou goest into the House of God, and draw nigh to hear, for much better is obedience than the victims of God, who know not what evil they do.* Mary who sat at Jesus' feet, and heard His word, *chose the good path, not to be taken from her,* and showed afterwards the constancy and increase of her love and wise devotion, when in the house of Simon the leper, she *anointed, with precious ointment, the feet of Jesus, and wiped them with her hair.* Let the profession of faith be proved by works of loving obedience in the daily life.

64.

The life of a christian may be truly described as the life of God produced and maintained in a human being. God (we are told) *created man in His own image; in the image of God created He him.* The life of a christian, if a true and right life, is the reproduction of the image of God in a fallen and corrupt creature. What a privilege to be invited to partake of this life! What a weighty thought for each of us: "God reproducing Himself in my soul." The Saviour says of himself as man: *I am in the Father, and the Father in me*; and through Christ this is equally true of us, if we, as new creatures in Him, are *members of His body, of His flesh, and of His bones; for whosoever shall confess that Jesus is the Son of God, God dwelleth in him, and he in God.* God subjects His infinity to the limitations of our poor humanity. If we are really what we profess, Catholic Christians, we carry God about with and in us, in our houses, chambers, streets, as well as in our churches. What a motive to watchfulness! what encouragement to faith and hope, and love of God, and of our neighbour; to the cherishing of the Holy Spirit; for *hereby we know that He abideth in us by the Spirit which He hath given us, and we have received the Spirit of God, that we might know the things that are freely given to us of God.*

65.

There is an observable and instructive resemblance between the record of Adam in Eden, and the story of the life (if it was faithfully written) of probably each of us. Can we not trace back our first great fall into evil and guilt, to some early, simple, and perhaps childish trangression? The desire of something forbidden, and the going after it, was the starting point of our sins. As we lived on this evil strengthened in us, and darkened our state before God. We added remorse to suffering and shame. When young we feared not want, and dreaded no storm. The day's care was sufficient for the day, but distrust, and dread, and care, have grown with consciousness of transgression. As a twig or leaf, small as they are, show the nature of the tree, so a child soon shows the connection with fallen Adam. Blessed be God, there is another parallel fact, the headship of Christ! *As by the disobedience of one man, many were made sinners, so by the obedience of one man, shall many be made just.* A christian life proves us, poor and feeble branches, engrafted into Jesus Christ, the tree of life: " *I am the vine* (he says), *ye are the branches*, and it is true both as to soul and body, that as in Adam all die, even so in Christ shall all be made alive.

> Come kneel before His cross,
> Who shed for us His blood,
> Who died the victim of pure love,
> To make us sons of God.

66.

Gentleness and patience with others is a beautiful character of true piety. It is one of the fruits of that love of our neighbour, which is always joined with and springs from the love of God. Among the graces of holy Joseph's character, his forbearance and patient gentleness towards Mary under circumstances that would with most, not only cause anxiety and suspicion, but harshness of conduct, was one. Joseph exemplified what St. Paul writes: *Charity is patient, is kind, thinketh no evil, beareth all things, hopeth all things, endureth all things.* Oh! for more of this precious grace! how it might help to win for our holy religion its way with opponents and despisers! and the patient humility of Mary, is very deserving of our notice and imitation; keeping silence, and leaving it to God, in His time and way, to put an end to this heavy trial of Joseph and herself. *Behold the handmaid of the Lord, be it unto me* (she said) *according to thy word.* Let their conduct and spirit be a lesson to us, not to allow the trials which God may send us or suffer to come to us, through others, make us fail in charity towards them, or submissive faith in Him.

67.

There was a rich man, that had a steward, and the same was accused unto him that he had wasted his goods. The parable, of which these words are a part, may remind us that every human being is a steward: from the Queen down to the lowest person this is true. If we lose sight of this fact we waste goods that are not our own, but our Heavenly Master's. Some waste property, some abilities, some health, all which, property, abilities, health, are given to us, to use, as stewards, for one end, God's glory. How many waste time, which should be made the most of, hour by hour, as men sip strong liquors, drop by drop ; as the waste of time goes on on earth, it is made a matter of accusation before the Lord of Life, in the courts of Heaven. Oh, let us remember this! Very great is the waste of grace. It is worse than the waste of money, or abilities, or health. For it costs more, and it can do more. It was earned for us by Christ's blood. How sad is the waste of opportunities of prayer! of instruction in God's word! of Sacraments! Every opportunity of these is a property of which we are stewards, and how solemn a thing that is, we shall only know when we die and go before God, *to give account of our stewardship.*

68.

A truly Christian life is not a mere release from punishment, or a mere passive acceptance of mercy. It is that sort of life in which the depths of our own sinful hearts are very fully fathomed, and the power of that love of God which redeems and sanctifies us is also fully explored by us. It is a real experience of two opposites: sin, our own sin, and grace, the grace of Christ. The opening chapters of the Bible bring before us, in the garden of Eden, man as a sinner, and God as a Saviour. They unfold the relation between Adam and Eve, after they had believed the Devil's lie, and the blessed and righteous God, who undertook the deliverance of the fallen and guilty. This relation continues still, and makes your life and mine, if we let it, more than a troublous dream, a blessed journey into a land of eternal rest. If Eden was lost to us through sin, Paradise is opened to us through faith and hope in Christ. When

God talked with Adam in Eden, and imposed on him the threatened penalty of transgression, death, He also, in the promise that *the seed of the woman should bruise the serpent's head*, took on Himself the burden of our trials, temptations, and even death, to open to us, and guide us into, eternal life. In the following of this guidance is the true life of a Christian: Go forth, each morning, in the remembrance of this, abiding with and influencing you in all your lawful duties.

69.

The recurrence of a festival of the blessed Mother of our Lord should make us observe how little value we should attach to worldly grandeur and distinctions. Mary was descended from a long line of kings, many of them potent, wealthy, and of great note in their day; but she was espoused to a working man, a carpenter, earning his and her food by daily labour; too poor to secure for her a lodging in the inn of Bethlehem, so that when she brought forth her divine Son, she laid him in a manger of a stable, where were the ox and the ass. So passes away the fashion of this world; so little connection with earthly dignity has the grace of adoption and of the Sonship of God. Happy are we if learning, in whatever way God teaches us, and in whatever state of life, that His presence with us, and in us, is our truest honour; that to have that relationship to Christ, and His blessed Mother, which the Holy Spirit gives, is a dignity as much above that of any worldly distinction as it is more inconceivably lasting. Earthly distinctions are but for the brief day of this life, but the sons and daughters of God in whom His Spirit dwells shall inherit eternal life. It is true wisdom to keep this in daily mind; and our Lord's words, *I give unto them eternal life, and they shall never perish.*

70.

Holy Job speaks thus of many in his days, that *they say to God, Depart from us, we desire not the knowledge of Thy ways,* and St. Paul says the same of the heathen, that *they liked not to retain the knowledge of God.* And is it not too true of numbers now all around us? How many young men, and women, who have been brought up to know God, as having made, redeemed, and called them to be His servants, and keep His commandments, do not choose to retain that knowledge? They prefer to have their own ways, and to follow their own wills. They love this world, its sins, pleasures, and pursuits, better than Jesus Christ, and His Gospel. They deliberately act wrongly, yet knowing quite well what is right. Therefore God, justly angry, often lets them go on in their wilfully bad courses, till perhaps they become reprobate and lose their souls. Let our care then be, daily to use our knowledge of God, as our God and Father in Christ, for our growth in grace and preparation for death, judgment, and eternity. Thus we shall not only keep our light from becoming darkness, but it will shine more and more, in our words, and works, our tempers, and whole conduct, unto the perfect day. What a blessing that will be!

71.

Am I am dog that I should do this great thing, was the objection of one when told by a Prophet of God of the great cruelties he would commit, especially on women and children. He could not suppose of himself that he would be so bad. Observe hence that it is merciful in God to discover to us gradually, as is His way of dealing with us, His children in Christ, the evil of our own hearts. If we saw and knew it all, from our early youth, we should be apt to become reckless of good conduct, and despair of salvation. As the cares of life, the temptations of the world come upon us, we learn, by sad experience, what weak, fallible, sinful creatures we are. Happy if, as we come to know this, we know also, practically and experimentally, where to go for help to meet care, and overcome temptation. Happy, if we go perseveringly to Jesus, as to Him who is *able and willing to save to the uttermost all who come to God by Him*. Be not cast down by any fresh discovery of the wickedness and deceitfulness of your own hearts, but see in it, a call from God to prayer, to watchfulness, to humility, to regular attendance on the means of grace, to faith in Him, who having shed His blood to open to you the kingdom of heaven, will not fail to aid you effectually, to walk on in the narrow way to it. *He that endureth to the end shall be saved.*

> There are briars besetting every path
>   That call for patient care;
> There is a cross in every lot
>   And an earnest need for prayer;
> But a lowly heart that leans on Thee
>   Is happy anywhere.

72.

The daily life of a servant of Jesus, is a work of faith, requiring gracious strength of heart, decision of will and character, and much resolvedness of purpose. *I will go forth in the strength of the Lord* (said a Saint of old), for in His strength only, as he well knew to have added, can I be strong. Look to Him then to go forth with you, day by day, into the world, and to add fresh grace to grace already received. Keep in remembrance through the day, your resolutions and vows of the morning. Especially watch against being dazzled by this world's vain allurements. Let them not prevail to turn you aside from the path of upright Christian duty. Beware of its delusive dreams taking hold of your mind and affections. By your baptism you renounced it, and as a professed Catholic Christian, you are already separate from it. Keep yourself separate, if not in your worldly calling and duties of life, in the dispositions of your heart. Bear in mind that you are to stand forth in daily life before others, in your duties, trials, and recreations, with the cross of Christ laid on you. It is a blessed distinction to be a soldier of the Cross, but it involves duties and trials, watchfulness and self denial, in common and little matters, as well as in rarer and greater. Often lift up your heart to your heavenly Father, for grace, amid worldly labour, when you are called to it; for an unworldly heart, amid earthly joys, if you have them, and for a spirit of self denial at all times. *If any man will come unto me*, said Jesus, *let him deny himself, and take up his cross daily, and follow me.*

73.

We ought not to dissemble our convictions, nor hide our faith from those who seem desirous of information and instruction. Christian charity, and the love of our neighbour, should make us *ready to satisfy every one that asketh you a reason of that hope which is in you, but with modesty and fear.* But Christian wisdom and discretion will keep us on our guard as to those who only enquire to abuse or contradict, making a mockery of sacred things. *Give not what is holy to the dogs* (said our Lord to his disciples) *neither cast ye your pearls before swine, lest perhaps they trample them under their feet, and turning upon you, they tear you.* Charity and prudence, zeal and discretion, are graces that have each their separate claims and duties, and which need not clash. Malignant and profane, and thoughtless gainsayers of religion, sometimes demand such a severe reproof, as our Lord gave the Pharisees, when He said, *why tempt ye me, ye hypocrites?* So St. Paul reproved Elymas. But for such poor fallible creatures as we are, the forbearance of silence, will as a general rule be our safest course when among those gainsayers and mockers, who seek occasion against Christ and His gospel. *He that ruleth his spirit* (Solomon says) *is better than he that taketh cities,* and *there is a time to keep silence and a time to speak.*

74.

There is a motive, too little regarded in general, that should influence us to zeal and earnestness in our profession of religion and attention to the duties they claim from us, namely, the good and comforting influence that our Christian conduct may have on others. *They shall comfort you* (said God by the Prophet Ezekiel), *when you shall see their ways and their doings,* so unlike those of the ungodly and careless, which brought the visitation of His wrath upon Jerusalem. It is very encouraging to the timid, and the weak in faith, and to beginners in a religious life, to observe a neighbour constant at church and Holy Communion, acting consistently with Catholic Christian profession in the daily walk of life, *fervent in spirit, serving the Lord, rejoicing in hope, patient in tribulation, instant in prayer,* in short, *fruitful,* as there is opportunity, *in every good work.* A Christian life is an effective teacher to a large class: to them especially, whom youth, or defective instruction, or natural want of resolution, or powerful temptations, or severe trials, call to be scholars, and to tread in the footsteps of others. St. Paul, after saying, *I seek not that which is profitable to myself, but to many others, that they may be saved,* adds, *be ye followers of me, as I also am of Christ.* We may preach Christ and His gospel to others, by a Christian life and conversation, even more effectually than by conversation or sermons.

73.

What a gift to our world is Christianity, if men understood it rightly, and properly valued it. It would be for the happiness and peace of nations as such; for the well-being of all classes of mankind; of kings, and rulers, and subjects alike, to be under the rule of God, and the influence of the gospel, and the Church of Christ. Whence come wars and fightings without, and all their frightful sorrows? Whence come revolutions and riots within a land, with all their various and manifold evils, but from ignorance, or at least as often, from disregard of Christian truth. If men *rendered to God the things that are God's,* loving service and obedience to His commandments, they would not fail, so often as they do; to *render to Cæsar the things that are Cæsar's,* loyal submission to the powers that be (and there is no power but of God), and to laws and authorities. St. Paul writes, *Render to all their dues; tribute to whom tribute is due; custom to whom custom; fear to whom fear; honour to whom honour. Fear God, honour the king,* are put in close connection by St. Peter. And it will be the wisdom as it is the duty of every true Catholic, to act daily on the admonition of St. Paul, *I desire first of all that supplications, prayers, and intercessions, and giving of thanks, be made by men for kings and all in high stations, that we may lead a quiet and peaceable life in all piety.* At this time there is much cause for our solemn attention to these admonitions.

76.

When God spared the Ninevites on their repentance, Jonah was very angry, and full of fretfulness. He blamed God, and said, *It is better for me to die than to live.* He could not endure to be little thought of. Is there not much of this very wrong spirit in us? We don't like to be of small account, and little esteemed. We are not indeed called upon to make ourselves despised, which has been the mistake of some holy men and women, but when we are contemned, and little regarded, let us consider: FIRST— How our dear Lord was so treated. *He was despised and rejected of men. He hath a devil*, they said, *and is mad, why hear you him?* NEXT: Do we not deserve to be little esteemed by God, by holy angels, by saints, perhaps by our fellow-worshippers, and our neighbours? If so, why are we angry because men in general do not esteem us? AGAIN: If the secrets of our hearts were fully laid open to others, who would or could highly regard us? ONCE MORE: To be despised and of little esteem is a slight touch of His cross, which Jesus gives us, and any conformity with Him is a blessing that will have a full recompense. Only let us take heed that the little esteem, the contempt, and reproaches of men, come to us, as it would have been Jonah's case, for our obedience to God's commandments, and our firm, open, consistent attention to His will. *If any man suffer as a Christian let him not be ashamed, but glorify God.*

77.

Though there is no presumption in an endeavour after a clearer sense of our own state of acceptance with God, yet it may be a safer course for us to restrain our curiosity of looking into God's Book of life, and to look into our being within the confines of salvation, by the revelation we base of it from within. Let us look into the real and internal proofs of the new nature in our own souls, and into what we have of the mind of Christ. It will be more advisable for us to see into the crucifying of our own wills, the mortifying of the animal life, the dying to the world, and its vanities and seducing follies, and from perception of the divine life within us, to gather a sure pledge of immortal life and happiness. For let us be well assured that the essence of these is a perfect conformity of all the powers of our souls, with the will of God. There is no better way to gain and keep a well grounded assurance of the love of God than to overcome ourselves and our own wills. Yes, he who finds Christ, *the Sun of Justice*, risen in the horizon of His own soul, *and health in His wings*, chasing away the mists and darkness of self-will and wrong affections, has no need to pry into the secrets of Heaven, for he finds the salvation of God transacted in his own soul, a throne set up there, and Jesus thereon reigning. He finds the Kingdom of Heaven within him, the Holy Comforter being to him a sure earnest of the eternal inheritance, and a *sealing unto the day of redemption*.

78.

It seems a design of God, as regards his saints, that there should be in their distinctive and characteristic graces, a deficiency, which even more than those graces marked out His own adorable and Divine Son to be the alone Saviour and Redeemer of sinners. Patient endurance of heavy suffering was the characteristic distinction of Job; but how faulty was it! what impatience mixed with and overshadowed his patience. Faith, producing eminent obedience, marked Abraham's life. But how defectively! In two recorded instances faithful Abraham shewed distrust of God, even to wilful falsehood: and if in Joseph's forgiving love we find no recorded failure, yet we find in him an early vanity that called for long and deep correction as a slave and prisoner. The meekness of Moses suffered an eclipse, *when they exasperated his spirit, and he distinguished with his lips.* So David, so Solomon, and Elijah and Hezekiah; so Peter the courageous, and St. John, the loving disciple, had recorded failures of temper or conduct. And these saints failed in their characteristic graces. So that this result is to be much noted by us, that while the Old Testament Church, expecting the promised Saviour, as the excellencies of her own witnesses to God's power and love came upon her, might say, " Like these will He be when He comes," there would be cause to add, "far above them all must and will He be" Their foreshadowing of Him is but faint and faulty. None of them can be He: not one, nor all of them together, are sufficient to stand between God and sinners as the *Mediator,* and *so as to put His hand upon both.* All these saints shewed themselves sinners. But He though *once tempted in all things like as we are* was *without sin. Being consummated He became, to all who obey Him, the cause of eternal Salvation.* So perfect and sufficient a Saviour is Jesus. Daily bless God for Him.

79.

Life is yours (writes St. Paul to the Christians of Corinth) *for all are yours.* A true Christian, while he

F

has natural life, lays hold on eternal life. The former is to him a season of grace, the seed-time of eternity, and the longer he lives, the riper he becomes for Heaven. Surely this is both comfortable and instructive for us. The comfort of life is ours : *As sorrowful yet always rejoicing.* Let your present life be overcast with clouds, or vexed with storms of trial, yet if there is any comfort on earth, you have it; your present life may be weak and failing, but your spiritual life as a Christian, ministers comfort to your natural life as man. Observe how true this is: poverty often clouds and eclipses the comforts of life; but *hath not God chosen the poor in this world* to be *rich in faith,* and *heirs of His kingdom?* If one humbles the other lifts up. Reproach is sometimes an heartbreaking trial. *My heart* (says the Psalmist) *expected reproach and misery.* Yet here is a Christian's comfort : *our glory is this, the testimony of our conscience.* What is man's condemnation, if God acquits? Worldly losses are often very heavy: yet we read, *ye took with joy the being stripped of your goods, knowing that you have a better, and a lasting substance.* Thus we see that the spiritual life distils comfort into the natural. There is no heavier grief to a Christian than sin, his own sins; yet his tears are both sweeter and more profitable than the triumphs of the ungodly. *A fool will laugh at sin;* but *as the crackling of thorns under a pot, so is the laughter of a fool.* Thus you see that *life is yours.* In the life of a Christian at its lowest ebb, there is a spring-tide of comfort.

80.

Life is yours (writes St. Paul to the Christians of Corinth), *death also is yours;* a great addition to be placed among the *all is yours.* There is a great fulness of truth in these words. Observe this at present, that to a true and earnest Christian, death brings deliverance from sin. While we are in the body, what St. Paul writes is found the sad confession of most. *The good which I will, I do not, but the evil which I will not, that I do.* Or as Solomon says: *There is no just man upon earth that doeth good, and sinneth not.* Are not evil thoughts continually rising in our minds? Is not sin ever seeking a lodging in our hearts? indisposing us to do good, so that *to accomplish that which is good, I find not.* Is is not ever irritating to evil? *The flesh lusteth against the spirit, so that you do not the things that you would.* It was a beautiful remark of St. Anselm, on seeing a boy letting a bird fly up, and then pulling it down again by a string: " It is so with me, when I would fly up to Heaven by meditation, I find a string tied to my legs; I am overpowered by corruption." Now death pulls off this weight of sin, and delivers the soul of the Christian into a free service of God. Are any of you ready often to say, conflicting with sin and temptation to it, *who can deliver me from the body of this death? The grace of God by Jesus Christ our Lord,* both can and will break down its power, so that it shall no longer rule; but death will do more for you when Divine grace makes you a combatant against sin, death makes you a conqueror over it. These are beautiful lines over one fallen asleep in Jesus.

> "Brother, thou art gone before us, and thy saintly soul is flown
> Where tears are wiped from every eye, and sorrow is unknown;
> From the burden of the flesh, and from care and fear released,
> Where the wicked cease from troubling, and the weary are at rest."

81.

We learn from Holy Scripture, and the records of His servants both before and after Christ, confirm this teaching of God's Word, that it is His very frequent plan of dealing with them, to delay the desired answer of their earnest prayers for deliverance from temptations and trials. It was so in the case of His Beloved Son, our Lord and Saviour. *My God, my God, why hast thou forsaken me; far from my salvation are the words of my sins; O my God I shall cry by day and thou wilt not hear.* If this was the case, can any Christian wonder or should he complain of unkindness if God so deals with him? Be not cast down then, if you find it so, still less give way to unbelief. As one said, say to yourself, "hold out faith and patience." That 21st Psalm, which opens with that sorrowful cry of Christ (for it is in His person David prophetically speaks), passes on, after a little, into high praise and thanksgiving. *He hath not slighted nor despised the supplication of the poor man, neither hath He turned away His face from me, when I cried unto Him, He heard me.* And in the triumph of His promised glory, the Saviour declares the answer to His prayer: *There shall* be declared to the Lord a generation to come, and the heavens shall show forth His justice to a people that shall be born, which the Lord hath made. His church and gospel shall have victory. Even so will God your Heavenly Father declare His justice, His love, and truth, within your soul, O Christian, by making those very trials and temptations which now perplex you by their continuance, manifest tokens of His purpose of love to you, by their sanctifying results on your wills and affections, by your growth in grace, your progressive preparation for Eternal Life, your cherished communion with Him, your closer union with your Saviour.

82.

Those are very awful words to which I call your attention, and beg you to read at home, and think them over carefully: *The natural man receiveth not the things of the Spirit of God, for they are foolishness unto Him; neither can he know them, because they are spiritually discerned*. The *natural man*, a man in his birth state, as a fallen creature, unenlightened as to his mind, and unrenewed as to his heart and will, not only does not, but cannot receive, understand, approve, and bring home to his own acceptance and pursuits, spiritual truths, nor those good things God has prepared even in this life for them that love Him. Dreadful condition of loss and ruin! God, His saving truth, His blessed gifts, Christ-made wisdom, and justice, sanctification, and redemption, are only to be spiritually discerned, by the teaching of God the Holy Ghost in the heart and mind of the regenerated man. As our Lord said to Nicodemus, *Except a man be born of water and of the Spirit, he cannot enter into the Kingdom of God.* There is an inner discernment of God and Christ, and Divine things, differing in kind very much from a verbal knowledge and profession of Catholic faith. How ought this to put every one into close examination as to his own possession of the Holy Spirit. *They that are in the flesh, cannot please God. But ye are not in the flesh but in the Spirit, if so be that the Spirit of God dwell in you.* Observe that, *if so be*, and learn from it how much it should be your case, and your prayer, that you may have that spiritual discernment of divine things, which is the fruit of the Holy Spirit's in-dwelling. *For as many as are led by the Spirit of God, they are the Sons of God.* Think well on this, and rest not till you can in your experience understand that weighty, solemn declaration of St. Paul: *The Spirit beareth witness with our spirit, that we are the children of God.*

83.

The sacred rites and ceremonies of our holy religion, and attendance on the Sacraments, may be abused in many ways. Let me warn you as to two of these abuses. *First*: if you substitute in your heart reliance on your attendance on these in the place of Christ, and His meritorious atonement for pardon of sin and peace with God. *Secondly*: if you are not careful to follow after holiness and to make progress in grace. Neither of these abuses is uncommon. The profane sons of Eli thought that to bring the ark of God into the camp of Israel would ensure safety and victory over their enemies. The presence of that ark had wrought, by God's appointment, great wonders in former days. But it was not to be an object, as Eli's sons were making it, of superstitious reliance, while there was a neglect of godliness, of penitence for sins, and of the fear of God. Gather hence a warning against a reliance on and abuse of the most sacred gifts and institutions of God, which at all puts Christ the Saviour out of view or on one side, and is not conjoined with surrender of the heart to God, and with careful obedience to His known commandments. Your personal godliness is ever the object of your Saviour's survey and care *His eyelids try the just; and Him that loveth wickedness does His soul abhor. Be not deceived: God is not mocked.* Be close and frequent in your attendance on God's institutions in this Church, and specially at the Sacraments, but remember that, like the ark of God, close attendance on them calls for watchfulness and reverential care over your words, and ways, and hearts. Was not Uzzah smitten by God, so *that he died by the ark of God*, when without due reverence he took hold of it? Truly, an awful warning as to our handling of sacred things!

84.

You are sometimes disposed to have great hopes

that you will make a progress in a pious and godly life, and when it seems to be otherwise you are dejected and unhappy. You get discouraged in religion. But your view of what is progress would have been too low and confined if you could easily attain to it. You fall short not so much of what you did have, as of what you ought to have had in view, the true mark of a Christian calling. Beware even more of being lifted up by success in resisting temptations, overcoming difficulties, and bearing trials. For, remember that all strength for such success is from God through Christ, who *worketh in us to will and to do of His good pleasure. Be strong in the Lord, and in the power of His might*, and He will uphold and lead you onward. We are alas! very slow to learn what we should, from the commencement of our Christian course, have held fast with mind and heart, the ability and willingness of our dear Lord to *save to the uttermost all who come to God by Him*. Keep on in the strait and narrow way of consistent profession. Maintain prayer, public and private. Be constant at Holy Communion; walk humbly with God; meekly, watchfully, and lovingly with your neighbour. Prize your privileges as members of Christ's Holy Catholic Church. God will not leave you, if you do not leave Him.

85.

These are some wisely beautiful words of St. Theresa, which well deserve your attention: "Let me no more trust, O my God, in anything I can desire for myself: dispose of me as you please. This I desire, for all my happiness consists in pleasing you. And if you would please me, by doing all that my desire craves, I see that I should be ruined. How pitiful is the wisdom of man! and their providence, uncertain! Let me die to myself, and Another live in me that is greater than I, and better to me than myself. Let Him live in me and give me life: let Him reign in me, and I be His slave, for my soul desires no other liberty. How can he be free that is separated from the Most High? What greater or more miserable captivity than for a soul to break out of the hands of her Creator? Happy those who, with the strong ties and chains of the Divine love, find themselves thus fastened: for *love is strong as death.* Oh! that one could see himself already dead by its hands." Who of us will make this holy longing of this saintly woman ours? or join in what she added: "I had rather live and die in the purpose and expectation of life eternal, than possess all the creatures and their advantages. Forsake me not, O Lord, for I trust in Thee. Let not my hope be confounded, let me always serve Thee, and do with me what Thou wilt."

86.

However heavy and sore may be your temptations yet if you return to and keep in exercise the fear of God, and love of Christ, do not be greatly troubled. You will be advantaged by them in the end. There is more danger in living without that conflict, for the Evil One is then leaving you quiet. You will advance further in the true life of a Christian, with temptations, than without; provided you *be instant in prayer, watching in it with thanksgiving.* Our dear Lord conducts us by various ways into His rest, and for this *better are the wounds of a friend than the deceitful kisses of an enemy.* The world and our own sensuality will be used by the Devil to keep us in false peace, and in a slight external, decorous profession of religion. But our Lord has a great and true happiness in store for us, which He leads into by the permission of temptations. *Thus we shall know, and we shall follow on that we may know the Lord.* Great condescension of our Lord, so to keep us in earnest, so to excite us, and induce us to proceed with diligence. Keep ever in mind that your calling is to Eternal Life with Christ in Heaven, and if allowed present temptations, are a means for that blessed end, be courageous under them. Give not way to sadness or unbelief. *God is faithful, who will not suffer you to be tempted above that which you are able, but will make also with temptation issue, that you may be able to bear it.*

No profit can'st thou gain,
By self-consuming care;
To Him commend thy cause; His ear
Attends the softest prayer.

Give to the wind thy fears,
Hope and be undismay'd;
God hears thy sighs, and counts thy tears,
He shall lift up thy head.

87.

As sure as there is a God, so sure it is that a religion from God has only reasonable commands for reasonable creatures. No tempers can be imposed on us by way of test, and advance in godliness, which we might as reasonably be without, if not required of us. God can only will that reasonable creatures should be more reasonable, more perfect, and more like Himself, and consequently will enjoin us no duties or tempers of mind, but such as have this tendency and object. All His commandments are for our sake, and are so many instructions to be more happy than we could be without them. A truly Christian man is offended at the conduct of those who live without religion, not only for other reasons, but because they are opposing God who is goodness itself, in the desire and endeavour to correct the madness and folly of fallen man. Religion is our cure: God's merciful communication of such rules and discipline of life, as may serve to deliver us from the infatuation and ignorance of our fallen state. It is to teach us the knowledge of ourselves and all things about us, that we may know the true value of things, may discern our good and evil, and not be as idiots in our choice. For this reason God presses His instructions upon us with threatenings and terrors, and makes our acceptance of His salvation, of Christ, of the Holy Spirit, and His graces, and of all that is for the good and cure of our souls, such duties to Himself as He will punish our neglect of. It is not without evident reason that Solomon says: *The wisdom of a discreet man is to understand his way, and the imprudence of fool's erreth. A fool will laugh at sin; but among the just grace shall abide.* Consider this well for daily guidance, that if even the reason of man abhors such things as are in themselves abhorrent, how contrary to the Divine nature must be all sin!

88.

Pride, vanity, self-indulgence, covetousness, envy, and other corrupt dispositions of the like nature, call for more watchfulness, self-denial, and restraint, than the appetites of hunger and thirst; therefore, till we make our self-denial as universal as our corruptions; till we deny ourselves all degrees of folly and vanity as we deny ourselves all excess as to drink; till we reject pride and envy as we reject gluttony; till we are as exact in being truly humble and charitable, as we are in being temperate; till we watch against all evil tempers, as we avoid all sorts of sensual indulgence, we can no more be said to practice Christian self-denial, than he can be said to be just and honest, who only denies himself the liberty of cheating and stealing. And till we do thus seek to carry into effect in our own daily lives, our Lord's admonition, *If any one will be my disciple, let him deny himself, and take up his cross and follow me*, we shall make no progress in true piety, but our Christian profession will be a mixture of no one knows what; circumspect in eternal things, regular in our forms of devotion, but careless and negligent of our tempers and hearts, the chief credentials of true piety. Thus it will be, unless we lay the axe to the root of the tree; till we deny and fight against the whole corruption of our fallen nature, and of the world around us, and give ourselves up to the Holy Spirit of God, to think, and speak, and act, in accordance with that wisdom and purity of which He is the author, and will be the supporter and perfecter in us. *If you live according to the flesh, you shall die, but if by the Spirit, you mortify the deeds of the flesh, you shall live; for whosoever are led by the Spirit of God, they are the Sons of God.*

89.

There are men and women, professed Catholics, not immoral in life, nor altogether neglectful of a Christian conduct and attendance on religious duties, who make their worldly occupation an excuse for a disregard of the Apostle's words; *This we pray for, your perfection. Choked with the cares of life, they do not go on to perfection.* That great British Saint, Venerable Bede, " that singular and shining light" as one justly calls him, used to winnow corn and thrash it, to give milk to the lambs and calves, and to work in the bakehouse, garden, and kitchen. Yet for temperance, patience, holiness, faith, and love, charity, and humanity, self-denial, true self-resignation to the will of God, for all Christian virtues, he became an eminent servant of his Saviour. Why should not each of you? Why should not you die to the world, as he did, before you must die? Why should not you separate your souls from your bodies and earthly things as he did, before the time of your forced separation comes? He took especial heed not to let this lower and earthly world draw him into its embraces and keep him from rising aloft. He trained up his mind Heavenwards and sought to know God and to be strongly attracted by Him from earth and sensual delights and cares, to a love of His everlasting beauty and goodness. Why should not you, like Venerable Bede, seek to be so much disengaged in your affections from this world and what is in it, that when you come to go out of it, you may not look back and say, "Oh what goodly things I leave! would I might live a little longer among them," but get your hearts so crucified to this world, that it may be an easy thing to bid farewell to whatever is valuable in your eyes. Try to *use this world as if you used it not*, and that you may say as he did, "I desire to be dissolved and to be with Christ. Yes, my soul desires to see Christ my King in His beauty." Let not your worldly occupations be neglected, but let this blessedness be secured in the first place and at all consequences.

90.

St. Paul writes to Titus, "*Young men exhort to be sober.*" It is not sobriety, as opposed to excess in drink, but sobriety of mind, *sober mindeduess*, which is here meant. What is this? Certainly not the not being trifling, without a spirit of enquiry, or a desire of information, or a desire and aim to advance and to excel in what is useful; and as certainly it does mean the not being vain and scornful, hasty, ambitious, inflated, and immoderate in any even good and laudable pursuit. But much more is meant, of which I will touch on a part. No man can properly be *sober-minded*,—who does not consider the present life as transient and uncertain, and inseparably connected with a future and everlasting state of things. But all men, especially young men, are apt to act, talk, and think as if there was only the present life. Unless, therefore, this life is viewed as a mere passage to another, and every day's employment as connected with another, future and eternal life, and that as the day's employment is carried on in Christian faith and obedience, or not, so will be the future, eternal state, young men will not *be sober* in St. Paul's meaning of the word. *Sober-mindedness* will be conceit, and affectation, and hypocrisy, unless the necessity of Christian faith and obedience weigh on the mind, rest in the heart, and affect the conscience. Nothing will make a young man *sober* who does not often and seriously consider that he is here for a little while, and that his future, unbounded, eternal state is connected with his present conduct and temper, his faith or unbelief, his attention to or neglect of religious duties. While eternity is kept out of sight *young men* will not *be sober*, and it is the grace of the Holy Spirit in answer to prayer which alone can make and keep them so.

91.

I will add a little more on the question of *sober-mindedness*, as well as its importance, not only for young men, but young women. Temper gives a tint to conduct, and so to character, and so acquires for a young man or woman favour or disfavour. If the natural temper is quick, sharp, rugged, *sober-mindedness* softens it down. If naturally good and gentle, it habituates it, and checks tendency to easiness and pliancy. It forms *the mind that was in Christ*. Discretion attends sober-mindedness, which brings it to bear on small as well as great matters of daily life, such as employment of time, conversation, recreations, dress. Observe a giddy, flippant, talkative, idle, dressy, young man or woman, and you may at once see the want of discretion and judgment, which a *sober mind* would give and retain. More particularly as to the conduct of life, the being *sober-minded* is an excellency. A man acts with great advantage who is so, not precipitate and hasty, who knows how to regulate himself in a storm as well as in a calm, or very favourable winds. What advantage such an one has over the fierce or timid, the man who blunders, runs headlong, or stops when he should move on, having no self-rule, not *sober-minded*. Without this gracious quality a man may soon be a torment to himself, and to others, a trouble to society, to the church, and to his country. So as to recreation and pleasure, without *sober-mindedness* there is great probability that our pleasures if not evil and hurtful, will be muddy streams, tumultuous torrents, that swell and rush, and are past, with no good result. Lay to heart, therefore, young men and young women, the Apostle's exhortation, and if you really desire to excel in a Christian life, *be sober.*

92.

All approval of the truths and precepts of Christianity is worse than vain if it does not lead us to be earnest, devout, and practical Christians. If our daily lives are allowably at variance with the known will of God, it is hypocrisy to pretend to like it, or to pray *Thy will be done on earth, as it is in Heaven.* Profession of religion, without a change of heart, and newness of life, leaves us like those Jews, who went away wondering, from hearing Christ's words, and seeing his miracles, but not becoming his disciples; admiring but not believing in Him. What avails our admiration of Christ, if we don't imitate Him? Thy goodness, thy power, thy wisdom, O, my Saviour, are indeed suited to draw me to Thee, and to win me to a better and holier life, but I am conscious of a great disposition to keep back from such a life. I need the continual help of Thy grace, that I may be a *doer of the word, and not a hearer only, deceiving my own self.* Help me, that in the daily trials of a Christian life, in the struggle with temptations, and against the influence of an evil world, and the deceitfulness of my own corrupt heart, I fall not from following Thee. Keep through the day that prayer of David in your mind: *Order my steps in Thy word, and let not any iniquities have dominion over me.*

93.

Where the Spirit of the Lord is, there is liberty. This liberty of a child of God, is such a thorough detachment from earthly things, as to follow lovingly the clear will of God. One sign of the heart enjoying this liberty is the not being too much attached to what are called comforts, but meekly accepting the privation of them. We may desire, but not cling to them. A heart having this liberty will not be much disturbed if sickness or other causes hinder customary religious duties. It is the will of God, which best quiets the heart. Other results of this liberty are sweetness of spirit, gentleness and indulgence to all that is not sin, or leading to sin: also the having a temper easily moved to what is good and loving. He, who enjoys this *liberty of the Spirit of God*, will not be impatient when his inclinations are crossed, or his aims frustrated. Such an one will seek to make others happy in their own way, if that be not sinful. St. Charles Borromeo, who was a very precise, and even an austere man, mixed with the Swiss, his neighbours, even joining occasionally in their carnivals, in order to win them to religion and Catholic truth. A true spirit of liberty in him, did this out of charity, and because such seemed to him the will of God. It is a blessed spirit to be in; let us cultivate it, and pray for it. It is the Holy Spirit's operation in us.

94.

The sleep of Jesus, in the midst of that tempest, which came on a sudden on the little vessel in which his disciples were crossing the sea of Tiberias, may teach us to be calm and quiet under any trial, however heavy, that we may be placed in. *In your patience ye shall possess your souls.* Let this be as a rule to us. Our Lord knows the minutest circumstances that befall us. We are always under His eye and care, and so long as we keep there before Him in humble believing prayer, we are safe, and *all things shall work together for our good.* He will wake up for our help, when He sees it best for us to be freed from any trial. This life is a sea soon crossed ; calm and storm alternate during our passage, but the soul that has Christ cannot be wrecked and need not fear. *I sleep* (says the bride in the Canticles), *i.e.*, calm and quiet in trials, *and my heart watcheth* for the voice of my beloved knocking; praying in the spirit, watching unto prayer, to learn the will of God in the trial, and profit by it. *I will hear* (says David) *what the Lord God will speak in me; for He will speak peace unto His people, and unto His saints, and unto them that are converted to the heart.* Blessed result of calm and patient endurance of trial. Oh, good Jesus (let your prayer be), work it in us.

95.

One of the daily duties of the Jewish priests, was the burning of incense night and morning in the temple.

In holy scripture, prayer is likened to incense. *Let my prayer* (says the Psalmist) *be directed as incense in Thy sight.* God looks for it from us Christians. But how often is this offering of the incense of prayer omitted? How many hurry off in a morning, into the cares of life and the temptations of the world, without prayer, or with only an hurried form of words, uttered without earnestness or heart, without intention or thought, and it is scarcely, if at all, otherwise at night. What a contempt of God is this! What a loss to themselves! The spirit of prayer, in those who are seeking to live to God and please Him, will indeed go much beyond this morning and evening incense of prayer. It will burn on, like the lamps in the temple, without going out; though not always with form of words, or outward bodily devotion. As we *walk in the spirit,* we shall *pray in the spirit.* But negligence, as to private morning and evening prayer, is not only dangerous to the soul, but often the commencement of a sad fall into sin, of departure from religion and God, and of final ruin. A prayerless man or woman treads on the verge of the precipice of Hell.

96.

As of our own strength we are not capable of truly good works, great or small, in the service of God, it may be safest to attend closely to the lesser, leaving it to Him to call us to greater services or sacrifices, when He sees fit. Meanwhile, little duties come daily, and, indeed, hourly, within our reach, and are not less suitable for our progress in grace and holiness than the greater calls of service which occur but rarely. Indeed, we may profit more by the lesser, inasmuch as they tend less to feed self-conceit, and to war against humility. Moreover, fidelity in trifles, and an earnest seeking to please God in little daily matters, is a proof of true devotion and love. *He that is faithful in that which is least, is faithful also in that which is greater.* It is quite possible to perform very ordinary duties with so perfect an intention, as to serve God better than in higher duties, done with less uprightness and simplicity of purpose. We have only to contemplate the holy household of Nazareth, in the early life of Jesus, with Joseph and Mary, to realise this truth. Let our aim then be to please our Lord perfectly, in our clear daily duties and present trials, and to attain an abiding spirit of filial love to God, and simple dependence on Him.

97.

The Heavens shew forth the glory of God. But the fullest contemplation of them will convey to our minds a very feeble thought of that glory of God which is to be revealed to, and in those who attain to Heaven. *God hath prepared for them that love Him*, what St. Paul calls *an eternal weight of glory.* God cannot give more than Himself. He is the happiness of the ever blessed Trinity, and in Heaven the redeemed and sanctified will have the possession of this. They will possess God without disturbance, for they cannot lose Him.

They will love Him without interruption, for He will fill their spirits. They will behold Him without ceasing, for every moment will discover to them in Him fresh matter of joy. *Happy is that people whose God is the Lord*, and who having Him such now, are careful to retain Him. But let us not forget that to open Heaven to us, cost the life and death of the God Man, our Lord Jesus Christ. He did not think the purchase too dear: but willingly bore the cross, and its shame and torments for us Shall not we then strive after Heaven, and *give diligence to make sure our calling and election?* Let the bliss of Heaven be more the object of your thoughts: and say with St. Augustin, "O Lord, Thou hast made us for Thyself, and our hearts cannot rest till they rest in Thee."

98.

When we see any one walking on the slippery edge of a frightful precipice, or another put to sea amid rocks in a threatening storm, we look on them with anxiety and alarm, as in danger of loss of life. And is not any one who places himself without necessity, in occasion of sin, in as dangerous a position as regards his soul? Is he not risking his salvation? When the Devil is lying in wait around, and his own corrupt passions stirring within? Alas, the Devil is always strong enough for us, so that we have no excuse for aiding him with opportunities for giving us a fatal fall. God has not promised his help to those who dare to tempt Him. Is it not written, *Thou shalt not tempt the Lord thy God?* Let St.

Peter's denial of a master he truly loved, through reliance on his own strength, and placing himself in the way of temptation, be a warning to us. The grace of God is not so at our command that if we encourage our spiritual enemies to attack us, we shall be sure of victory. The case is quite otherwise. Avoid carefully then occasion of sin : keep firmly from bad company : shun watchfully all dangerous curiosity : restrain your eyes and ears while out in the evil world: dally not with temptations: imitate the holy and chaste patriarch Joseph, whose best weapon (St. Ambrose says) was his running away from danger. *He fled, and went out.*

99.

Consider that this life is given us as a preparation time for obtaining great graces needful for another and eternal life. Let us look upon the world, as we pass through it, in this light. Its sights of sorrows are to calm us, and to call out kind affections. Its pleasant sights are to try us, and produce self-restraint ; both are to excite our thankfulness to God. Let us endeavour to be as that angel who could descend among the miseries and mercies of Bethesda without any loss of his own purity, or equable happiness. Let us gain healing for our souls from the troubled waters we see around us. Make up your minds to have to sustain a certain measure of pain and trouble in your daily passage through life. This will, by the help of God, prepare you for it, and make you thoughtful, and patiently resigned, without preventing your cheerfulness. It will connect you with the saints of the Church, whose lot it was, with scarcely an exception, to be patterns, and admirable ones, of patient endurance, and this sense of association with them may bring you a special consolation. View yourselves as following Jacob, whose days were few and evil, and David, who in his best estate, was as a shadow that declineth, and Elijah, who despised soft raiment and sumptuous fare, and captive Daniel, who led an angelic life in an heathen land and a godless court, and be light-hearted and content, because you are thus called to be members of Christ's Pilgrim Church. Rejoice in this world, not so much because it is yours, but because it is not. *We also, having so great a cloud of witnesses over our head, laying aside every weight and sin which surrounds us, let us run by patience to the fight proposed to us, looking on Jesus.*

100.

God speaks of His people, by one of the old prophets, by the term *Jewels*. If true Christians are as jewels in the discriminating, all-searching regard of God, His grace must have wrought a great change in their hearts and natures. For all are born in sin, and have naturally evil hearts and corrupt affections, wills alienated from the will of God. St. Paul must have spoken truth as to the *jewels* of God. *If any man be in Christ, a new creature, the old things are passed away, all things are made new* Be not unconcerned, nor even uncertain as to this change in your own case. The thoughtless world derides the word *conversion*, but there is no matter on which each should examine him or herself more closely than as to your own present participation in this *new creature*. Rest not in hopes and good wishes, but be concerned to ascertain that God has created in you *a clean heart, and renewed a right spirit*. And as there is a day coming when God will collect together all His *jewels*, keep it in your minds and prepare for it carefully. Think of it as sure, fixed, and approaching. Improve the thought of it, to your comfort and support, under present duties, cares, and trials. *That which is at present momentary, and light of our tribulation, worketh for us above measure exceedingly an eternal weight of glory, while we look not at the things which are seen, but the things which are not seen; which latter are eternal.*

101.

Hail, full of grace. The Archangel Gabriel thus saluted the mother of Jesus, and we learn from the salutation how wonderfully God enriched her with His best gifts, and spiritual treasures. The brief record of her in holy scripture, shews her full of faith, of hope, of charity, of humility, of patience, of every virtue. *Blessed among women*, as mother of the Divine Redeemer, blessed in the singular pre-eminence of her holiness. Our contemplation of her should not be a barren one. They little honour Mary, however they may say with their lips, *hail, full of grace*, who are vain, dressy, full of love of the world, talkative, idle, busybodies, as wives disobedient to their husbands, as mothers negligent of their children, and as Catholics, *having an appearance of godliness, but denying the power thereof.* Are there not many such? Give God thanks, if he keeps you from the mistake of supposing that Catholic devotion consists in using any form of words, without surrender of the affections, the will, and the life to Him, and His commandments; such only are the true children of Mary, who seek, by God's grace, to resemble their blessed mother. The *hail, full of grace* of others, is too much like the words of Judas, who said, *hail, master, and kissed Him*, but the while betraying Christ.

102.

Reason thus, Christian, with yourself, " If God is the creator of my soul and body, my loving father, by whom I exist, and am maintained in this state of being, if I derive from Him, all I have, and look for what is truly good, why do I not rejoice and glory in Him? Why do I not seek to *love* Him as he demands, *with my whole heart, and soul, and mind, and strength?* Why do I not look with more indifference, not to say contempt, on all earthly perishing things? Why do I not *mind* more *the things that are above, not the things that are upon the earth?* Why do I not seek daily to realise that *my life is hid with Christ in God?* Why do I suffer so many vain cares, and desires to lord it over my thoughts, aims, pursuits, and actions?" Lift up the eyes of your soul, O Christian, to God; and keep Him ever in view. *Press towards the mark, to the prize of the supernal vocation of God in Christ Jesus.* Be not cast down by fear of what any earthly enemy, or even Satan, can do to harass you, seeing you have an Almighty Father in Heaven, and an equally Almighty Saviour and Brother, there interceding for you. Think with what confiding affection of heart David says to God, *I am thine, save me.* And reflect in your daily course: *If God be for me, who can be against me.* But *walk solicitous (or humbly) with thy God.*

108.

At one of the great yearly festivals of the Jewish Church, the Feast of Harvest, two loaves, the first fruits of the harvest of the year, made of the finest wheat flour, were presented before God as a sample or specimen of the whole harvest, and were waved by him towards the four quarters of the globe, as a solemn acknowledgment that all blessings in nature and providence, throughout the wide earth, come from Him. It was on this same festival day, above eighteen hundred years since, that the first fruits of the harvest of souls, redeemed by the precious death of Christ, were presented before God in the form of about three thousand converts to the faith as it is in Jesus. Like the two loaves these converts were a sample of what the grace of God could produce out of poor simple earth, out of fallen humanity.

They were a blessed specimen of the power of God, the Holy Ghost, and of the grace of the gospel. They were, we are told, *persevering in the doctrine of the apostles, and in the communication of the breaking of bread* (Holy Communion) *and prayers*. They shew us what professed Catholics should be in all the earth, and what should be our daily life. *I beseech you, by the mercy of God, that you present your bodies a living sacrifice, holy, pleasing unto God, your reasonable service*. It is the Holy Spirit alone, remember, who can lead, sanctify, strengthen, and daily renew us. He must dwell in us, to make us what we are called to be, the bread of God.

104.

Try your ownselves; if you be in the faith, prove ye yourselves, advises St. Paul. We may very easily set ourselves down as good Catholic Christians, when we are not. Self-trial is not a work we are naturally disposed to. And we seek more to be pleased by God in our religion, than to please Him. In other words, we are over anxious for comfort and enjoyment in our Christian profession. It is good then, sometimes to be alone, and having God present with us, to try ourselves as to the reality of our religion, and if our pleasure in it rests on a good foundation; to judge ourselves, not by pleasant feelings, but by accordance of our lives with holy scripture. Self-denial, bearing the cross, and doing and suffering the will of God, have more part in Christ's teaching than promises of comfort. God was with David and Hezekiah, and Job, and Jeremiah, and St. Paul, and His own blessed Son, in distresses, and in apparent low and desolate estate. Let us rest our hope, not on inward joy, so much as on God's word, on Christ's death and intercession, and on the Holy Spirit's aid, enabling us to walk watchfully, humbly, and holily, rather than comfortably. To be led out of ourselves to God in Christ, is the way of present and eternal soul safety.

105.

God has given us a law of perfect liberty. If we are God's children, we have the spirit of God; and *where the spirit of God is, there is liberty*. But we have this liberty, that we may (not abusing it) use it to God's glory, and in the service of Christ; setting aside self-will and self-rule. These are sure to lead us wrong, whereas while God rules us, we only need patient trust to be rightly led. Our Heavenly Father loves us more than we can love ourselves, and watches over us with an Almighty Father's love. Neither devil nor man can stay His grace from us while we retain our trust in Him. A true Christian has no cause to fear anything while following his Saviour's call and guidance to duty or trial As Jesus slept while the storm was tossing the disciples on the sea of Tiberias, so He may seem indifferent or regardless of what threatens to overwhelm us; but it is not so; ignorance, neglect, or indifference on His part as regards any of His people are impossible. Let our daily surrender to God be then hearty, willing, and unreserved; it will be with us as with David: *I walked at large because I sought after Thy commandments.*

106.

St. Paul reminds us: *You are bought with a great price; glorify and bear God in your body.* If we have an hearty and simple desire to do this, the result will be an unfailing and increasing happiness which nothing should disturb. There is no real happiness in this life where there is not a peaceful heart, and God tells us, *there is no peace to the wicked.* Even religious and devout people, who only half give themselves up to God and retain much self-will, only feebly realise this peace of God. They are easily disturbed by many things; by scruples, by dread of God's judgment, and by the changes and chances of life in this varying world. But he who gives himself unreservedly and submissively to God, will be more and more filled with His peace. *Much peace have they that love Thy law, and to them there is no stumbling-block.* And as we are prone to grow like to that to which we are closely united, the closer we cleave to God, the stronger, the more steadfast, and the more tranquil shall we become. They who cleave to this world are for ever tossed about with the waves and storms of uncertainty and insecurity. God alone is immovable, unchangeable, and whoso trusts in Him *shall not be confounded.*

107.

Christ said: *For judgment I am come into this world, that they who see not, may see:* very encouraging and comforting to those who, conscious of their ignorance, weakness, and corruptions wait with perseverance on God in prayer, to be taught His saving and sanctifying truth. Becoming as little children, they will go on and enter into the kingdom of Heaven. Are we such? Do we from our hearts cry: *Enliven me, and I shall keep Thy words; upon Thou my eyes, and I will consider the wondrous things of Thy law: if I have erred, teach Thou me.* Such shall be taught of God: *for the Lord is sweet and righteous; therefore will He give a law to sinners in the way: He will guide the mild in judgment: He will teach the meek His ways.* But Christ added: *That they who see, might become blind.* This is, indeed, an intimation of judgment to those who despise religion and the truths of holy scripture, as beneath their care and study; who never pray for the Holy Spirit, and think they can find the way to Heaven by themselves, by their own wit and wisdom. They become blind; and if they keep in such presumption and repent not, final spiritual blindness will settle on them. Let us be *poor in spirit, little in our own eyes. God resisteth the proud, and giveth grace to the humble.* He turns from those who are *wise in their own conceit*, but to them that have no might, He increaseth strength.

108.

There were six cities of refuge in the land of Israel, so called because any one who had killed another unintentionally, without malice, by fleeing into one of them was safe. They were like the sanctuaries in old Catholic times, places of safety, under the wing of the Church. No river rolled near them. They stood in plains, or level land. But there was a high hill, or eminence near them to guide those who sought to them. They were designed to shew us our escape in Christ from sin, its guilt and ruin. There is nothing to prevent our getting to Him. The way is plain and open, and while yet afar off, we may see if we will, that ensign of the cross, which once lifted up on Calvary, is still set before us in the Church and her sacred services. We may hear the invitation: *Turn ye, turn ye from your evil ways; why will you die? Come to me all you that labour, and are burdened, and I will refresh you.* And *him that cometh to me I will not cast out.* Let these invitations and promises rouse our faith, quicken our diligence, kindle hope and keep it alive. From the walls and battlements of Heaven, angels and saints have seen many escaping from the wrath to come. Do they see us? If you have cause to doubt it, delay not.

109.

It was God's promise by the prophet Malachias, that in every place there should *be sacrifice and a clean oblation offered to His name.* This promise has a fulfilment in the service of the Mass, or *the shewing forth the Lord's death till He come.* But is it not too true what God complains of against the Jews, that many regard this *table of the Lord as contemptible?* Else how is it that so many who might attend, keep away from this *clean oblation,* offered twice, or more frequently every morning in this Church? Our dear Lord, after his resurrection, made himself known at Emmaus in the breaking of bread. Is it not worth while to seek the presence of Jesus in your own souls? to have a visit from Him, by His Holy Spirit resting in your hearts? to get strength for the trials and temptations of the day, comfort and support in the cares of life, from some of which who of you is free? Our dear Lord is ready to meet with us, and is, doubtless, grieved that so few care to meet with Him. If ye seek to me, He says, *I will give you rest,* and He will be as good as His word. St. Francis of Sales says: It is impossible to seek the Saviour in a more precious, lovable, or blessed way than in the Holy Eucharist, if not by our own partaking of it, yet by being devoutly present when the Saviour's death is shewn forth at (as St. Paul says) *the table of the Lord..*

110.

There is one thing we all need more deeply and truly to learn, and live in a consciousness and a serious, though by any means not mournful remembrance, of: that all created and visible things are but shadows, passing shadows; and that God only, known and rested on in Christ, is the true, eternal, satisfactory, existing reality and substance. To live through the day, in this great truth, is to dwell on the borders of Heaven; it is to begin even now in this life, to pass from time into eternity, from mortality to immortality. In order to this, we must not be very anxious about what may be regarded as the husks of things, but seek to get to the kernel of that Divine life which Jesus is to all that seek to God by Him. *This is eternal life, that they may know thee, the only true God, and Jesus Christ, whom thou hast sent.* Be thankful to God if, from age or bodily feebleness, or sickness, or any circumstances, even very trying ones, you are at all removed out of the hurry of the world. The ball of life goes rapidly down the steep hill of time. Let us be wise, to embrace Jesus and His great salvation with our whole hearts; to trim our lamps, and to give ourselves daily afresh to Him, who gives himself to us, poor sinful dust and ashes, in His Son, and in His Holy Spirit, and in His appointed means of grace.

111.

We will do all the words of the Lord which He hath spoken, should be our settled resolution, as heartily declared, but more faithfully kept, than by the people of Israel in the wilderness. There was more than one great error in their case, but against one I will now warn you. It regards the motive of such a resolution, the principle it springs from, and the spirit in which it is acted on. Self-recommendation to God, or the notion that our own obedience purchases His favour, must be watched against. That something of truth mixes with this error, makes it more delusive. The alone sufficiency of Christ's merits is a first great truth of Christianity. *When you shall have done all these things that are commanded you, say we are unprofitable servants, we have done that which we ought to do.* All our obedience needs the sprinkling of the blood of Jesus. We must practice the resolution of the people of Israel on the principle St. Paul puts before us: *The charity of Christ presseth us; judging this, that Christ died for all, that they who live may not live to themselves but unto Him, who died for them, and rose again.* There is no principle of uniform persevering obedience to God's commandment comparable to this in purity, soundness, effectiveness, and truth. Other motives may do something, but let us be influenced by this principle, and to know the love of Christ for ourselves, not as a tale told which we cannot or dare not deny, but as a truth that concerns each of us, and is influentially felt by us. It is too true that we may go on in a decorous, respectable course of life, and yet never give our thoughts or affections, with any serious regard, to the work of Christ on the Cross, and now in Heaven for us.

112.

I will warn you against another error in your practice

of this good resolution : *We will do all the words of the Lord, which he hath spoken.* This is self-confidence, and a dependence on your own strength. What a warning against this error is St. Peter's denial of his Master! Yet we are prone to set about our duties in our own strength, forgetting that it is Heavenly help and grace alone which can make us efficient for any good work. Remember that *it is God who worketh in you, both to will and to accomplish.* Seek ever, therefore, the support of that Holy Spirit, promised to all who ask for it. Let not the help of God be unmeaning and formal words, but moving you to seek in faith, and with persevering earnestness, an essential as well as great blessing. Add, if not in words, in your heart, to your resolution of obedience and submission to God's will, "the Lord being my helper." Thus warned and instructed, go forward in the fulfilment of what God calls you to do or bear. If you seriously reflect you will easily find that you have such calls to action or patient obedience every day and hour of your lives, and to meet them in heartfelt, humble dependence on divine help.

113.

Behold (says God, by the Prophet Ezekiel), *all souls are mine.* Bring home to your own mind and heart that you have an immortal soul which belongs to God. You are not your own masters; you have been not only created, but bought with a price to be God's servants and property; that price, *not gold or silver, but* the precious blood of Christ. Let this be an abiding remembrance, for it may keep you, if prayerful and watchful, from not only sinning wilfully, but from carelessness and levity of life. It will help you to become, what I trust is your aim, the servants, or what is more, the sons and daughters of God. It is by looking on God as our God and Father in Christ, that we become like Him, and if we are like Him now it is a blessed thought that we shall one day *see Him as He is*, and dwell for ever with Him. This view of God, and of ourselves as His, aids to produce recollectedness, reverence, earnestness in religion, and an holy zeal, thoughtful, and persevering. It helps to sustain devotion, and a Godly life. *Whether ye eat or drink, or whatsover else ye do, do all to the glory of God.* Would that every one of us might watch to regulate his or her daily life, by such a rule, or, as the same apostle rather more largely admonishes the Colossian Christians : *All whatsoever ye do in word or work, all things do ye in the name of the Lord Jesus Christ, giving thanks to God and the Father by Him.*

114.

What blessed encouraging words to all who love and serve Him, are those of God by Malachias, *They shall be my special possession saith the Lord of Hosts, in the day that I do judgment.* If there is a day coming in which God will declare His people to be His special possession, His own valued property, His jewels, let us think much of it, and be ourselves every day preparing for it. Let us regard it as sure, fixed, and approaching; and let the thought of it be our support and comfort under present trials. Let us be assured that the dead in Christ are not lost, nor gone, because dead. We know not how near they are to Christ; how precious to Him, how blessed in Him; nor how great benefactors they may still be to us, in their prayerful remembrance of us. The Church continually bids us remember some of them, who counted not their lives dear to themselves, that they *might finish their course with joy*. Though we may not be called to be martyrs, we are called to be saints, and in a loving service of Christ, and a daily holy life, to be *followers of them who through faith and patience inherit the promises*. Let us keep in mind, all through the day, that God claims us now; that we are not our own, but belong to Him; and so let us glorify Him with our bodies and spirits which are His, and have been *bought with a price* to be His *special possession*.

115.

Some persons are alarmed and disquieted by supposing that when a bad thought comes into their minds, they sin. This is an error. We sin only when we dwell with any complacency on bad thoughts; when we entertain and do not reject them. If we have not given occasion to the entrance of a bad thought by indolence, by self-indulgent habits, by negligence in guarding our senses, *i.e.*, our eyes and ears, and if we absolutely repel it, a thought, however bad, will rather bring us favour from

God, and increase grace to us. We must not expect, in this life, to have a peace that is without combat. Holiness does not consist in being exempt from temptation, but in standing firmly against it. Be not afraid then of thoughts which in spite of yourselves come into your mind; but, as quickly as possible reject them; driving them off, as you would a wasp or gnat. Have recourse at once to prayer. Say to Christ, *Help, Lord, or I perish*, and He will help you to triumph against your assailants. *Resist the devil, and he will fly from you*, and it may be, that angels unseen, sent by God, will come and minister to you a present blessing.

116.

When your hearts have wandered from the blessed Shepherd's side; when your affections have become entangled in the world; when your faith has failed, and foot slipped, instead of cherishing an evil heart of unbelief, return at once to *the fountain open for the washing of the sinner*, and plead that precious promise: *Return to me and I will return to you, saith the Lord*. The charity of Jesus never faileth, *and though you should trespass against Him seven times in a day, and seven times in a day shall turn again to Him, saying, I repent*, He would forgive you, for this is the rule by which He instructs us to walk towards those who offend us; and in this, as in all things, He gives the example, that we should follow His steps. The utmost breadth of the *New Commandment is, that ye love one another as I have loved you*, and therefore the extent of our duty to others, as laid down by Him, is the strongest encouragement to our confidence in Him as regards ourselves. Remember, then, that under whatever circumstances you may apply to Jesus, there is *ground for everlasting consolation, and good hope in grace*, since the perfect holiness of His nature, the entire conformity of His heart to the law of God, and his unfailing truth, renders it morally impossible that He should *in any wise cast you out*.

117.

One chief hindrance to growth in grace, and in love of God, is self-love. Thereby Satan gets and keeps an hold over us. Human respect, a regard to what others say and think of us—that fatal snare to souls—springs from self-love. All God's dealings with those whom He leads on in a true spiritual life tend to root out of our hearts this evil, poisonous weed of self-love. In proportion as it is weakened, and our wills bowed to God's will, hindrances to our progress in godliness disappear, many troubles and conflicts which harass our spirits vanish, and our souls have abiding peace and tranquility. But we only perceive this dangerous self-love by the light of God's Holy Spirit, opening out to us the secrets of our own hearts. We scarcely realize how much this evil rules in us, till God, by humbling trials, assaults it and seeks to tear it away. If we then co-operate with His teaching, a true love of Him, of His will and laws, His word and people, and ordinances, will fill the vacancy; we shall, in some good measure, realize the blessing of the *pure in heart* and *see God*. The promise of Jesus will be made good to us: *My peace I give unto you: not as the world giveth do I give unto you.*

118.

The Lord's field is the world, in which He has His children who are the good seed: and there the Devil has also his cockle, the ungodly. They are two great armies, under two great and powerful leaders, as has been the case from the very first. But the field is also the heart of each of us; particularly and individually, in which our Lord if we will let Him, is now seeking to sow the good seed of His grace, that he may bring forth fruit unto God; while the Devil on his part is alert to spread the seed of vice, and disobedience to God's commandments. But as he cannot make himself master of our hearts without our consent, he seeks to insinuate himself into us unawares, and to that end is watchful to seize on any time and occasion in which he finds us less or not at all on the watch over ourselves. What a motive for each to keep in mind our dear Lord's warning: *Watch ye and pray, that ye enter not into temptation.* Let not carelessness, nor assumed security, cause us to slumber, seeing that we have an enemy so powerful, so active, so vigilant, to effect our ruin. *Watch ye, stand fast in the faith, do manfully and be strengthened.*

119.

It is by no means easy to clear ourselves out of the meshes of self-deceit. The cockle bears a sufficient resemblance for a time to wheat, to give us warning that under the semblance of a grace or virtue there may be what is very opposite. We may mistake our timidity in the profession of religion for meekness; our impatience of opposition for zeal; our indolence for patience; our covetousness for prudence; our keeping back from self-denying duties for humility: Satan transforms himself into an angel of light; we must use against him self-examination, with earnest, honest prayer. *Prove me, O Lord, and try me, burn my reins and my heart.* We easily become unreal in our Christian profession, and keep up a show of Christianity with little true fruit of grace in the daily life. We are as the fig tree on which our Lord found only leaves. Let us look at and up to God: pass over to Him with sincerity and earnestness in our spirits, wills, and affections; lean on Him, as our Father in Christ (blessed sanctifying thought), and seek that the love of Christ may turn out of our hearts the love of self, that noxious occupier of the fallen man, and then we shall become more real and sound in our profession of religion, more truly gracious and good in spirit and conduct, and withal more peaceful and happy Christians.

120.

The maintenance of thankfulness of heart to God has

much to do with our growth in godliness All true progress in the religious life is closely connected with the love of God. *He that abideth in charity abideth in God, and God in him.* And this charity or love is the cause and effect of thankfulness. What light and air are to plants, that, the belief and sense of God's presence and favour, is to Christian graces. They grow thereby. A spirit of thankfulness leads us to see mercies we should otherwise overlook: it enables us to appreciate more our daily and common blessings. While we magnify God and thank him for all his goodness, our hearts are enlarged, and when our *hearts are enlarged, we run the way of God's commandments* (as David says), where we only walked or crept before. We feel a liberty in well-doing and in great self-denials we did not feel before: because the spirit of thankfulness brings home to us at once the height of God's goodness, and the depth of our own unworthiness. Let us cultivate more than we do the spirit of thankfulness, and make thanksgiving more a part of our daily devotions. *Let the peace of God rejoice in your hearts, wherein ye are called, and be ye thankful*

121.

It must be manifest to all who take any note of their own hearts and conduct, that there is a great and grievous inconsistency between their public walk, and their private devotion. Few are in the world, what they are in their secret chambers. In these, they get near to Jesus. They find it good to be there. They are willing at times to say, *I am ready to go with thee to prison and to death.* But scarcely are they come abroad, entered into company, engaged in business, than they seem to be removed to a distance from their Saviour; at best, they follow afar off. What is the cause of this? It is in a great measure want of recollection. Prayer is to some a regular act at certain times, not the habit of the soul. We do not carry a spirit of watchfulness and supplication into the ordinary concerns of life; we are not sufficiently careful to keep in public and outward life, the advantages we have gained in private. Nor is it easy; for if *the spirit is willing the flesh is weak.* Let this lead you to frequently lift up your hearts to the Lord, even amid your worldly occupations. Let me advise you to pause, if it be but for a few moments, to breathe out a prayer to Him, who alone *is able to keep you from falling.* One mainspring of a true Christian life is the habit of returning to Jesus, by frequent and short intervals. Do not fret and be disquieted, when you have wandered from the Saviour's feet, as though it were a vain attempt on your part to keep there, but calmly and humbly resume your place, trusting in Him to receive and keep you. But be not one person in your chamber, or in church; and another in your family, your work, or your shop, and with your friends.

122.

The High Priest of the Jews, when engaged in one, and that most solemn office, wore the vestments of an ordinary priest. Observe now that herein he figured out our Lord Jesus Christ, especially when making atonement upon the cross for the sins of the world. St. Paul reminds us of this: *He emptied himself, taking the form of a servant, and in habit formed as a man, he humbled himself, becoming obedient even to the death of the cross.* Yet as the Jewish High Priest was in his greatest glory when engaged in the special offices of that great day of atonement, so was our Lord and Saviour most glorious in His great humiliation on Calvary, and when *crucified* through *weakness*, He redeemed us by His atoning death, and so be assured that we are never more truly exalted than when we are bearing the cross of self-denial, or of any trial and suffering for His sake. *If you be reproached* (says St. Peter) *for the name of Christ, you shall be blessed, for that which is of the honour, power, and glory of God, and that which is His Spirit resteth upon you.* Let us not turn aside then from the cross of trial, however humiliating and painful, though hard to bear. Only draw, and keep nigh to God. Happy shall we be, and happy are we now, if we truly rest on Christ and His most precious blood as shed for us. It is by trials and sufferings that we are perfected. If we are valiant in the conflict with sin, the world, and the Devil, we shall win a crown brighter (far beyond all words can describe) than the brightest that monarchs wear, of gold and gems of great price.

123.

All true servants of Jesus Christ have at times to

endure contempt and rebuffs from others, and to shew meekness and lowliness of spirit. David in one of his Psalms characterizes the worldly and the ungodly as *persecuting the poor man and the broken in heart.* Bear this trial *heartily*, when it comes on you, *as unto God.* It is a feature of true Christian humility to accept, even thankfully, such trials when they come before us. We are never to go out of our way to seek them. This is an error. But we are to be patient, submissive, calm, under them. The meekness which makes least show is the truest and most genuine fruit of the Holy Spirit. Beware of speaking haughtily and sharply when tried and rebuffed by any. Though it is natural to us, as I dare say you feel, it is unbecoming a disciple of the meek and lowly Jesus. While we crush down angry and impatient feelings, and strive to keep (it is not easy) calmness and a peaceful, loving mind, we need not let such feelings trouble us much. Though they may recur and last the day through, by prayerfully striving to keep them down, we shall be growing in grace. The Lord is drawing us to Himself as the sheep of His pasture—*my sheep hear my voice, and I know them, and they follow me, despised and rejected of men.*

124.

We have great opponents of the grace of God in our own bodies. We must all know and feel this. Accustom yourselves, therefore, every morning, to caution your souls after somewhat this manner: "Take care,

O my soul, diligently to watch that body thou art dwelling in, and all its actions and all its suggestions. In whatever is contrary to the will of God, or will displease thy Heavenly Master, Christ, oppose it and subdue it, till thou recallest and rejectest from thee all sinful desires, all corruptions and affections." Make it thy care, O Christian, that it may be with thee as with that blessed apostle who says: *I chastise my body and bring it into subjection.* And every night thus question and examine your soul: "O my soul, hast thou this day subdued thy body, that rebel against thy Lord and Master? Hast thou kept it under and restrained it in the pursuit of worldly pleasures? Hast thou dealt with it watchfully and severely?" If you persevere in such exercise, you will so regard the body as a dangerous companion, that you will praise God for His grace, given to keep it under the soul. You will say with St. Paul: *Thanks to God, who giveth me victory through our Lord Jesus Christ,* to whom be praise for ever and ever.

128.

Our Lord Jesus Christ came not to revolutionize human nature, but to make it truly noble and holy. He would have us learn that eternity is not so much a future state, to which the stream of time is bearing us on, as a present but unseen state, and that in fact we have all now entered on eternity. It is around us now, and we can none of us get out of it. We have begun, and must go on living for ever. And God is not a being, dimly thought of, separated from us above our heads, in the far off blue sky, but not far from any one of us, the Maker and Ruler, in whom we live, and move, and be, and if we will receive Him as such, the Father, who has so loved us as to give His Son to live and die on the cross for us. Christ teaches us that the service God would have us render Him is humble, loving obedience. It is by this, and not by keeping up outward forms and ceremonies, and profession of true faith, that we go on towards that eternal life, which what we call death will not introduce us to, but perfect as something already begun. *My sheep* (said Christ), *hear my voice, and they follow me, and I give them* (it is, indeed, now given) *life everlasting.* Would that all of us, and all around us, laid this well to his heart. Worldly and irreligious men and women are dying already, in eternal death. "*She that liveth in pleasures is dead while living.*" But the same St. Paul would have us to say: *Whether we live or die, we are the Lord's.* This is eternal life begun; make haste, and take care to secure it.

126.

The final end of every one who wisely perseveres in using the grace of God, shewn towards him in the redeeming work of Christ, is to be with God and with Christ for ever. *Father* (said Jesus), *I will that where I am they also whom thou hast given me may be with me, that they may see my glory.* Let our daily life, then, be an ascension towards this blessed result. *For-*

getting those things that are behind, and stretching forth to those things that are before, let us press towards the mark, to the prize of the supernal vocation of God in Christ Jesus. St. Paul thus bids us to follow him in his ascension to God. Personal religion is the application of Divine truth, the doctrines, precepts, spirit, and grace of Christianity to ourselves. And it is to be a kind of ladder, by which our souls are to move on and upward towards the enjoyment of eternal union with God. We may look back and look round to see how it has been and how it is with us, and bless our Heavenly Father for His preserving love, and say with humble thanksgiving: *By the grace of God, I am what I am;* and praise Him, that *His grace in me hath not been void.* But let us be ever looking and moving onward and upward. *Employing all care, minister in your faith virtue; and in virtue, knowledge; and in knowledge, abstinence; and in abstinence, patience; and in patience, godliness; and in godliness, love of brotherhood; and in love of brotherhood, charity.* And as you pass now from this Church, pray that God may keep these His own words in your thoughts and purposes, words and ways, throughout this day, and while in a world which puts them out of sight and thought.

127.

Without faith it is impossible to please God. Without that union to Jesus, which faith maintains, we have no spiritual life in us. It is not the profession of a creed, nor of all Catholic truth, nor the maintenance of forms and ceremonies, nor repetition of prayers, but an inward power operative on the whole spirit and life, and bringing the will, affections, aims, and conduct, into obedience to Christ, in which consists the true faith of a Christian. Cherish it, if you have it; seek it at once, if you have it not. Blessed, for ever blessed, be that mother's child, whose faith has made Him the Son of God. The earth may shake, the pillars of the world may tremble, the sun may lose his light, the moon her beauty, the stars their glory, but as for that man that trusts in God what shall move his heart, alter his affection towards God, or the affection of God to him? No; he can say, *I know whom I have believed.* I am not ignorant whose precious blood has been shed for me. I have a shepherd, full of kindness, full of care, and full of power. Unto Him I commit myself. The assurance of my hope I will endeavour to keep as a jewel unto the end, and by care and labour, through the gracious mediation of His prayer, "*Keep through thine own name, those whom thou hast given me,*" I shall keep faith, hope, and charity, and be kept.

128.

We must be careful not to confound the working of our feelings with true Christian Faith; a frequent mistake. Thus, when a near relation or valued friend dies, there are few who are not then open to the impressions of religion. There is a seriousness, and a tenderness of spirit. Fears, wishes, thoughts, resolutions, pious words, that would have had no place at other times, are ready at hand. Ungodly Balaam said, when his feelings were stirred, *Let my soul die the death of the just.* Such persons stand by the grave, or bedside of the dying, and weep: or when alone, think of God, of Heaven and Hell: say some prayers, perhaps, or listen to, or join in religious conversation. Some are affected by sermons, and seem moved as others are by a band of music: or as crockery vibrates before a strong wind, or as cards shake on a table. They come out and say "How much they felt under the sermon—what good it did for them." Now they do believe at the time; but it is with a faith with which the Holy Spirit of God has not much to do. They feel, but it is nature, rather than grace, that is at work. Their feelings soon calm down into previous indifference, or worldliness. They are like dram-drinkers, who mistake temporary excitement for health and strength. Let us guard against this delusion. The proof of true faith, and genuine religion, is perseverance in obedience to the will of God.

129.

If he commit any iniquity (said God of David), *I will correct him with the rod of men.* This, and many other words of God teach us that, however sorry and reluctant God may be to afflict us, He will not spare a single stroke of chastisement so long as we cling to evils which degrade us, and will be the death of our souls. And they also teach us that the design of God in judging and afflicting us is merciful; that He has no pleasure in our suffering; that he intends to separate the evil in us from the good, to perfect us, and fit us for eternal blessedness. If we love evil in any form, or habitually do what is wrong, though we may hide our evil habit from men, we cannot hide it from God: nor can we evade those searching judgments by which He seeks to free us from our bonds of evil. And when the visitation comes, and the divine judgment is searching us through and through, let us learn and remember that God is not so much angry with us as with the evil that is in us: that He loves us, and because He loves us would make us quit our evil. Let us learn and remember that He will and can only remove His judgments from us as we remove from ourselves our sins. *Cease to do perversely, learn to do well* (said God in His judgment), *then, if your sins be as scarlet, they shall be made white as snow; if red as crimson, they shall be white as wool.*

130.

The hearer of instruction from the word of God, who receives what he hears in a sincere and earnest heart, and seeks to hold it fast, will have to *bring forth fruit in patience.* This is both a most valuable and a most difficult attainment, for to wait is usually harder than to work on and obey. *The husbandman waiteth for the precious fruit of the earth.* To become a good and truly profited hearer; that is a good doer of the instructions received from Holy Scripture, requires long and much patience. But the longer we wait with perseverance in prayer and watchfulness, the more excellent will be the spiritual result, as regards our own state before God and growth in grace. For God *is not unjust to forget our work and labour of love.* If we persevere according to patience in good work, laying to heart what we learn, and bringing it to bear on our daily life, turning it, so to speak, into use for the regulation of our own Christian temper and conduct, we shall certainly reap the benefit. We shall *grow in grace and in the knowledge* (that most blessed knowledge) *of our Lord and Saviour Jesus Christ.* Be patient, therefore, in well doing; be steadfast in every good word and work; establish your hearts before Him *who has called you unto His kingdom and glory.* Hold fast what you receive of instruction in the truth of God, and it will not be lost upon you; but the evil one and the world are always at hand to get it from you.

131.

Our Lord and Master, Christ, when on earth, among other mercies, *leaving us an example to follow His steps*, stopped, on one of His journeys, at a city of the Samaritans called Sychar. There, wearied with the walk and the noontide heat, *he sat thus by the well side*, near the city, and, thirsty, he asked of a Samaritan woman, who came to draw water, *Give me to drink.* And He improved the occasion to converse with her and to in-struck her and her townspeople, who at her invitation came out to see that stranger, who, though a Jew, had not shunned but sought them; in that salvation He came from Heaven to effect and teach. When the woman said, *I know that the Messias cometh, who is called Christ: when He cometh He will tell us all things*, Jesus said with holy dignity, *I am He who am speaking to thee.* Now, these Samaritans were very ignorant, separate from the then (the Old Testament) Church of God, and very hostile to the Jews, as these were to them. But our Lord sought them, conversed with them, and blessed them. He stopped with them two days. Hatred, contempt, and prejudice were not in Him. And thus He gives us a lesson not to despise or stand aloof from any because they are ignorant, or not of our Church, or may show dislike or hatred of us and our religion. Be kind as you have opportunity to every one. Seek to do every one good, by word and act, and thus to win and gain them over to the best way, the service of God our Saviour, *who will have all men to be saved, and to come to the knowledge of the truth.*

132.

When our Lord in His journeyings *came to Nazareth, where He was brought up, and went into the synagogue according to His custom on the Sabbath day*, and read to them from the book of Isaias the prophet, and applied what He read, they not only rejected His words with scorn and anger, but thrust Him out, and even sought to *cast Him headlong* from the precipitous hill on which their town was built. Awful hardening of heart! But let us learn a lesson of warning not to rest in our privileges as Catholics and Christians, as if the having them will suffice to make and keep us right before God and in His favour. These people of Nazareth were members of God's Old Testament Church; they had a synagogue or church; the Law of God and the Scriptures of the Prophets, probably the Psalms of David; and met for the worship of God on Sabbath days. But their hearts were not given to God: and He did not, and does not, approve of any service while the heart is far from Him. They were full of conceit, pride, and prejudice. They had known Jesus living among them as the son of the carpenter Joseph and the poor and lowly Mary; and they despised Him, and hated His plain spoken truth. We must not rest, let all remember, in the outsides, which are but the shell of piety. God looks for the kernel, and says to us, *Give me thy heart.* When we keep this back, and rest in profession and privileges, God may leave our hearts to rest in our evil passions. Let our earnest daily prayer be: *Let my heart be undefiled in thy justifications, that I may not be confounded.* Mark the difference between the ignorant and erring Samaritans, who received and believed in Jesus, and the proud and prejudiced Nazarenes, who rejected Him and drove Him from them.

133.

Though it is a dangerous deception to rest on outward

privileges, in the profession and forms of piety, it is not less so to neglect the use and improvements of those privileges, of the Sacraments, of public worship, and of opportunities of instruction. When the people of Nazareth drove Jesus away, *the Galileans received him, having seen all the things he had done at Jerusalem, on the festival day; for they also went to the festival day.* They had left their homes and worldly callings, and journeyed some distance, with both trouble and cost, to worship God on some sacred occasion (it matters not what) of the assembling of devout Jews at Jerusalem, and they had a recompense in not only seeing the works of love and power which Jesus then wrought at Jerusalem, but being so moved by all they saw and heard, as to welcome his visit to their neighbourhood. Observe then that those who neglect God's house and worship, little consider of what a blessing they may deprive themselves. *Draw nigh to God and he will draw nigh to you*; is His our engagement. What greater blessing can anyone have, than the earnest, deep, longing of his own heart to know Christ, or what more blessed than to have experience in his own soul of the ascended Saviour, *that he is able to save for ever them that come to God by him.* If that most awful word, *you will not come to me that you may have life*, was true of them of Nazareth, of the Galileans that most sweet promise would be true, *him that cometh to me, I will not cast out.* May this influence us to *expect the Lord and wait for him*; and our expectation shall not fail. And mark, how much we may learn from these historical records of Holy Scripture and of the earthly life of our

Lord and Saviour. How much they lose who neglect these Scriptures.

134.

We read that Jesus said to Thomas, *Because thou hast seen me, thou hast believed; blessed are they that have not seen, and have believed.* Christians, like Thomas, are found, in whom, amid the strugglings of unbelief and the conflicts of a doubting heart, a real love of Christ lies deep within. And this, as it is His gift, is known to the Lord. If any such be here now, there is comfort and hope for you in this record of Thomas; for there is this encouragement for you, that your Saviour can subdue the evil heart of unbelief and disperse the doubts and questionings that rise up from it like noxious vapours, and give such power to the love he has imparted, that it, feeble as it may be, shall rise up over every hindrance, and produce a blessed confession of Christ, in the daily life. The once doubting, questioning, and weak Christian shall go forth with gracious strength before the world, *leaning on the Beloved*, and avowing him to be *my Lord and my God*. And there is this further instruction for all, that if any one comes to Christ honestly, he will in nowise be cast out, be his imperfections, his ignorance, his deficiency in faith and grace what they may. Only come, and persevere, in the spirit of him who cried *Help mine unbelief*, and you will not be turned back by Him, Who *will not break the bruised reed, nor extinguish the smoking flax.*

135.

It is one thing to fall into little venial faults, through the frailty of human nature, and another to commit them through culpable negligence, and want of watchfulness. To speak now of the first only. A man falls through frailty who, while ready and desirous to renounce and avoid what he knows it is according to God's will he shall keep from, yet through some slight impatience of spirit, or excitement, or levity, or too much talking, thinks, or says, or does what he should not think, say, or do, perhaps is more mirthful than is meet, or over-anxious and busy about wordly matters. Now if as soon as he recovers himself he grieves that he was not more guarded and watchful over his own heart, and inwardly and truly abhors all sin, and hastens to confess his faults to God, and seek pardon, his transgressions will not be imputed to him as heavy, for his heart, through the grace of his Saviour, is not wilfully and allowably corrupt. He hates that which is evil; sin has not dominion over him. Nor will such faults, so dealt with, hinder his growth in grace, and progress in the kingdom of God. This reflection may comfort and encourage some.

136.

We are told in Holy Scripture, at its commencement in the Book of Genesis, that *the Spirit of God moved over the waters.* The Spirit of God signifies the Holy

Spirit, the Holy Ghost, the third person in the Blessed Trinity, who thus took part in preparing our world, or globe we are on, to be the habitation of man. It proves His power, and His co-operation with God the Father and God the Son, for our well-being in this life. He co-operated to make man in His own image, and so the Holy Spirit co-operates still to fit us for eternal life, and restore that image in us. He keeps down our corrupt inclinations, reduces into order pleasing to God our natural appetites and dispositions, subdues our will to God's will, forms and cherishes, and causes to grow our graces; and brings and enables us to use our talents, whether many or few, for the glory of God, of Christ, and the good of our fellow creatures. He makes each of us, if we will let him, a *new creature in Christ Jesus.* Yes. Observe it is, if we will let him. Many will not let Him, but grieve Him, resist Him, and drive Him from them. Let none of us so sin against God the Holy Ghost and our own happiness. Cherish this Holy Spirit by prayer and watchfulness. Keep in continual mind that: *If by the Spirit you mortify the deeds of the flesh, you shall live; for whosoever are led by the Spirit of God they are the sons of God,* and often say:

> Come, Holy Ghost, our souls inspire,
> And lighten with celestial fire;
> Thou, the Anointing Spirit art,
> Who dost Thy sevenfold gifts impart.
> Thy blessed unction from above
> Is comfort, life, and fire of love;
> Enable with perpetual light,
> The dulness of our blinded sight.
> Keep far our foes; give peace at home;
> Where Thou art guide, no ill can come.

137.

Only seek and endeavour to serve Christ honestly and heartily, and you will have shown to you more and more, in your daily experience, his care over, and his watchful love for you. You will find that there is invariably one way by which He will prove this to you, that this world becomes not so attractive to you, as once it was, and that while you can still enjoy any blessings and comforts it may, through the mercy of God have for you, you are becoming less attached to it. The more your own souls find a sweetness in religion, and in communion with God, the less worldly satisfactions will have hold of you. Who can keep up the intercourse of his soul with the ascended Jesus, and yet cling to the vanities of the world and of life? All must endure them, and in some degree all of us have somewhat to do with many of these trifles and empty pursuits. Else, as St. Paul says, *you must needs go out of this world.* But if we strive and pray, that He who has so true and perfect claim to our most loving affections, Christ, may have it, and that our wills and aims and desires may be subject to the claims of his truth and grace, He will not fail to answer such prayers, and to bless such endeavours on our part. It is a rich mercy when our dear loving Lord brings us to live less and less soiled and injured by the sins, follies, and vanities we see around us, and more entirely His people.

And if some things I do not ask
In my cup of blessing be,
I would have my spirit fill'd the more
With grateful love to Thee;
More careful not to serve Thee much,
But to please Thee perfectly.

138.

A single dead fly or other insect, will be likely to spoil a pot of sweet ointment, and to make its owner put it aside. To be a *sweet savour to Christ*, who has bought us to be His, is our calling as Christians. Is there not something that hinders this, and is likely to render all our religious profession and service unacceptable to Him? We shall find it, if we watch ourselves; easily, too, may we find it, and very often. This is self; self-esteem and the desire of others; this is the dead fly, that spoils our service, both of God, and our neighbour. In preaching, what Priest may not detect this spoiling evil, this dead fly? In almsgiving, in daily intercourse with others, in conversation especially, who can deny its continual presence in his heart? Did not Jesus say of Himself, *I seek not my own glory?* But, which of us can truly say so? And did He not blame the Pharisees; *all their work they do to be seen of men?* Let these His words guide and warn us—We should pray much, and be on our guard against this very besetting sin. What are we? vile, corrupt creatures; sinners, pardoned and accepted of God, through the merits of another, and without whom we can do nothing truly good. Let the recollection of this make and keep us humble and meek. *Where humility is there also is wisdom.*

139.

There is a pleasing story told of an Italian bishop, who derived much of his happiness from looking up to Heaven, with the reflection that his chief business *here*, was to find how he could get *there*. And such is the worthiest object of a Christian's consideration. When family distress or other calamity comes upon us, then we fly to religion for our refuge, because then convinced of the impossibility of finding consolation elsewhere. How much rather ought we to devote our best powers to the service of the God who has redeemed us, when he has made our hearts light with joy and blessing, and when our faculties are not impaired with grief. *Seek him while he may be found* is advice often inculcated. We should seek Him to instruct us, by prayer. We should seek His will in His revealed Word, and we should seek His grace, to enable us to live according to His Word. We have every encouragement to ask, for it is said: *Knock and it shall be opened unto you.* We are warned to *be sober and vigilant; to watch and pray.* In the Bible, we have advice suited to every circumstance; and how diligent should we be in making ourselves acquainted with those Scriptures which were *written for our learning, and can instruct us unto salvation by the faith which is in Christ Jesus.*

> Our hearts, if God we seek to know,
> Shall know Him and rejoice:
> His coming like the morn shall be,
> Like morning songs His voice.

140.

It may reasonably be expected that, since you desire happiness and your own true and lasting welfare, you will choose and follow after what will give you the most solid, refined, and lasting happiness, and abandon whatever is inconsistent with it and opposed to your real well-being. True piety is a source of such happiness. That piety which some think will put an end to all enjoyment, and therefore keep at a distance from; that Christianity which some may tell you makes men unbearably precise and strict, and dead to all life's enjoyments, will give you a happiness more pure, noble, and lasting than all this world can find for you. Religion not only proposes to us future blessedness beyond the conception of any one, but gives present happiness beyond what they know who are strangers to it. The happiness of being at *peace with God, through our Lord Jesus Christ*, of a quiet, approving conscience through the conflicts and trials of daily life; communion with God the Heavenly Father; the graces which God the Holy Ghost forms and nourishes in the soul, such as faith, patience, hope, love, gentleness, kindness: these are part of the present enjoyments of true piety. *As it is written, that eye hath not seen, nor ear heard, neither hath it entered into the heart of man, what things God hath prepared for them that love Him.* If these words are true as to this life, much more as to the life to come. Hesitate not, delay not, to secure for yourselves that *peace of God which surpasseth all understanding.* Jesus will give it you if you honestly and heartily ask Him.

141

All you are children of the light and of the day. Is it so indeed with us? Is it day within us as well as without? The sacred light of the truths of the Gospel, and of the Church are around us, and without, but to us there may yet be darkness. The glory of God in the gift of Christ, the exceeding riches of that Saviour's love, in the provision for all our spiritual wants, the evil of sin, the vanity of this world, and the great realities of the world to come, may not be rightly apprehended by our minds, nor affect our hearts, nor influence our lives. If it be so with any, remember that awful declaration: *This is the judgment, because the light is come into the world, and men loved darkness rather than the light; for their works were evil.* But some of you, I doubt not, have not only day without but within you. *God has shined in your hearts, to give the light of the glory of God in the face of Christ Jesus. Blessed* then, *are your eyes for they see.* This day is but the dawn of eternal day, to be enjoyed in Heaven. You are hastening to a world, where God Himself shall be your light, and *there shall be no more night.* Be earnest therefore; humbly and prayerfully watchful, to *walk as children of the light*, in your intercourse with others; and *so let your light shine before men that they may see your good works, and glorify your Father who is in Heaven.* Do not sleep as do others, but *watch and be sober.* Let not God find you idle, but busy in what is good, both as to the work of His grace in your own soul, in Christ's Holy Catholic Church, and in all with whom you come into contact.

142.

St. Theresa compares the soul to a castle, of which prayer is the gate, and in the principal court of which God dwells, or seeks to dwell. God says to the owner of this castle, *give me thy heart.* As there are many who go round the walls, without entering into the castle, so there are many Christians who never enter into themselves, nor look into their own souls, nor search how it is with them. They are not residents in their own castles, and know little or nothing of what passes in them. As in a well kept and occupied castle, there would be a discipline observed, essential to order and safety, so it will be with a true Christian as to the keeping of his soul. As faith might have her residence within the embattled courts of nobles, and sacred services kept up, and holy lessons taught and heard, and acted on, so assuredly will it be with the soul of a true servant of God. He keeps his soul for God his Saviour, as the loyal and true-hearted nobleman kept his castle for his sovereign. St. Theresa was first led to those thoughts of that perfect surrender to God, which marked her character and life, by observing her own uncle in his castle, dividing his time in prayer, holy reading, and the occupations of rural life. He kept the castle of his own soul with diligence. *So may you, employing all care, minister in your faith, virtue, and in virtue, knowledge, and in knowledge, abstinence; and in abstinence, patience; and in patience, godliness; and in godliness, love of brotherhood, and in love of brotherhood, charity; for if these things be in you and abound, they will make you to be neither empty nor unfruitful in the knowledge of our Lord Jesus Christ.*

143.

You desire to make your Lord some acknowledgment

in your daily life for His death and Passion, to Him so bitter, to you so salutary. It was the desire of a very saintly servant of Christ, Gertrude; and this, she tells us, was His teaching: "When you follow another's interest in preference to your own, you make me some acknowledgment for my captivity, when in the morning of my Passion, I was taken, pinioned, and grievously tormented. When you humbly acknowledge yourself in fault for anything, it is an acknowledgment for the judgment, when at the first hour I was accused by false witnesses, and sentenced to death. So when you refrain your senses from what delights them, it is an acknowledgment of my being scourged at the third hour. When you obey an ill-natured superior, you acknowledge my crown of thorns. When being the injured party you ask pardon first, you honour my carrying of the cross. When you go almost beyond what you can in charity to others, you honour my sharp endurance of being distended on the cross at the sixth hour. When to hinder a sin you endure scorn, contempt or reproach, you acknowledge my death and its humiliation for the salvation of the world at the ninth hour. When being reproached you answer humbly, you, as it were, take me down from the cross. When you prefer your neighbour to yourself as more worthy of honour, or other good thing, than yourself, you repay me for my burial. We may learn, hence, how we may thus daily and hourly *put on the Lord Jesus Christ*, who for us *humbled himself, becoming obedient unto death, even the death of the cross.* It may be very profitable to us, spiritually, to follow the instructions of this saintly woman.

144.

Beware of taking too narrow a view of what is meant by *the world*. It is not confined to any actual intercourse with society. We carry it about us: into our retirements, our houses, our retreats, our churches. Being in us, it fastens on spiritual things, and will manifest itself through them as an inner spirit. It comes out in the love of rule, in self-pleasing and in self-complacency, in jealousies, in desire of praise and love of notoriety, and esteem from others. And it may thus transform outward piety into what is only another shape of worldiness. *Remember Lot's wife;* though holding on to the skirts of her husband, too conscious of danger and evil to remain in the wicked, voluptuous city, yet too inert of soul and irresolute in heart to hate it and forsake it utterly, looking back upon it with a lingering fondness, she was turned into a statue of salt. It is a marvellous illustration of the difference of a life, ever on the watch and striving against the world, and one carelessly yielding inwardly to it and its various allurements. Oh! the great grace of that faith which hesitates not to struggle and keep down the strongest tendencies of our nature that are adverse to God's will as set before us in Holy Scripture. Such self-denying, world renouncing faith sanctifies what is pleasing and joyous when it ministers to the glory of God, or endures crosses, *despising the shame*, in view of a closer conformity by them to the image of Christ.

148.

We read of the Patriarch Isaac, that he went forth *to meditate in the field.* When you have opportunity imitate him, and leaving the busy town, the work of man, the haunt of sin, go forth, and mounting some eminence look around you, where hills and vallies, parks, pastures, and cornfields meet your view on every side; or walk through some wood or by some river side, and drink in the air poured round you in spring and summer, and listen to the joyous notes of various feathered songsters; or go into gardens and delight your senses with the perfect beauty and delicacy of form and colour, and the sweetness of the flowers you find there. Thus, when you have ranged through sights, and sounds, and odours, and your heart warms into joyousness, and with your voice seems full of praise and worship, reflect that all you have seen and observed is but a very poor and dim glimmering of the glory of the Maker, your God and Father in Christ. Such is He in His eternal uncreated beauty that, if it were given us to behold it, the rapture of the sight would exceed our present power to sustain. When Moses said to God, *Shew me thy glory, He answered, thou canst not see my face, for man shall not see me and live.* But that mere reflection of God's glory which you may have by observation of created nature, and by thought and meditation, will be sufficient to sweep away gloomy and desponding thoughts, and a sadness which opposes your own growth in grace and your Christian usefulness to others. *Let thy works, O Lord, praise thee, and thy saints bless thee.* It is well written:

> O God, O good beyond compare,
> If thus Thy meaner works are fair,
> If thus Thy bounties gild the span
> Of ruin'd earth, and sinful man,
> How glorious must the mansion be,
> Where Thy redeem'd shall dwell with Thee!

146.

Confession completes penitence. It is the first instinct of a truly filial heart. No sense of sin, its guilt and shame, has reached its depth, till the wronging such a Father, wounding His heart, grieving His love, is felt to be the blackest feature of it. While the soul stands off from God, conscious of sin, but saying inwardly, "I repent, but I will not confess," the core of sin is there. The poison is in the wound still, and will frustrate the cure. A true penitence for sin against a Being, and God is such, will lead us to that Being, whose forgiveness and the restoration of whose confidence and love are essential to our peace. God seeks to expunge that rancour of the soul, which is the real venom of the wounds of sin, and that passes not out till the penitent, hungry, footsore, tearstained, travelworn, falls at his Father's feet and cries, *Father, I have sinned against Heaven and before Thee; I am not now worthy to be called Thy son.* Confession re-establishes the filial relation, which alone gives to penitence its perfect fruit. While that relation is withheld the Father's heart is unsatisfied, the child's spirit is unsoothed, or deceptively so, the heavenly home is closed, and its songs are still. But let the barrier which a sullen heart holds against God be removed, let inward shame, and fear, and sorrow, break forth in David's confession: *Have mercy on me, O God, according to Thy great mercy, and according to the multitude of Thy tender mercies blot out my iniquity. I know my iniquity, and my sin is always before me. To Thee only have I sinned, and done evil before Thee.* Then the pardon pronounced over the penitent will be ratified. *The Lord has taken away thy sin. This, my son, was dead, and is come to life again; was lost, and is found.* Who now among you will not listen to the Church's invitation, and take advantage of her call to you to come to her confessional? Let not the Sacramental love of Christ be thrown away by any of you.

147.

Redemption by Christ is the spinal cord of the Bible. Every promise of God in the Old Testament is built on facts, especially one great fact, developed in the New. From first to last it is *God in Christ, reconciling the world to Himself, not imputing to them their sins, and Him that knew no sin, for us He hath made sin, that we might be made the justice of God, in Him.* It is God in Christ, treating with man, every when and everywhere. On the basis of the atonement completed on Calvary, God meets with man, and pleads with him in that promise: *If your sins be as scarlet they shall be made white as snow; and if they be red as crimson, they shall be made white as wool. If you be willing, and will hearken to me, you shall eat the good things of the land.* Strike out the record of the

Passion and Death of the Incarnate word, and there is no meeting point of man and God. God would not have pronounced forgiveness; man could not believe in it; nor could Heaven rejoice over it. But now, God, as a Father, taking man as a penitent to his bosom, quickens, renews, and saves. A new heart he can and does give, and a new life. The soul made anew after the image of the Saviour, to be born at length, through all the travail and sorrow of present discipline into the sunlight of the eternal world. The carrying on and completion of the work of redemption in man individually is the office of the Holy Ghost, the Paraclete; a promise of God, resting for fulfilment on the atonement of the Son, as the Son Himself assured us. I will ask *the Father, and He shall give you another Paraclete that may abide with you for ever. I will not leave you orphans; I will come to you.*

>Eternal One, Almighty Trine,
>Since Thou art ours, and we are Thine,
>By all Thy love did once resign,
>By all the grace Thy heaven's still hide,
>We pray Thee keep us at Thy side,
>Creator, Saviour, strengthening Guide.

148.

Envy, as a daughter, follows Pride, her mother, and hinders our thankfulness to God for His mercies. Comparing our own things, or times, with those of other men, or times, instead of giving thanks for what we have, we are apt to repine that it is not with us as it was, or is with others. While our eye is thus evil, because God is or has been good with others, we shall neither have tranquility of mind nor thankfulness of heart. Let us rather look on our own things, and remember that what we have, comes of His unmerited bounty, and what we have not, may either have been justly forfeited by our sins, or mercifully withheld for our good, to keep us from that entire contentment in this life and this world which might prevent our pursuit of a better world and a life to come. It may also be well for us to compare ourselves with those who have less, and to remember that the very poorest and most desolate may serve to us as a glass wherein to discern God's greater bounty to us, and as objects for our sympathy, tenderness, and as we are able, our charity. And as for past times, we shall do well to consider how many of God's children there have been, in our own and other countries, who would rejoice and sing if they enjoyed a small part of that prosperity in outward things, and that liberty of serving Him, and confessing Christ in His Church, and Sacraments, and sacred ordinances, which we have. *Godliness with contentment is great gain.*

149.

God makes use of mercies and chastisements as tests of character, not for His instruction, *for he knoweth the very secrets of the heart*, but for ours, for that of others around us, and of the church at large. When Christ gave Peter and his fellow-fishers *a very great multitude of fishes*, so *that their net brake*, it brought out Peter's faith and humility, for such was the purport of his prayer when he *fell down at Jesu's knees, saying, depart from me, for I am a sinful man, O Lord.* When great mercies and blessings come to us, either unexpectedly, or as a return of our own honest endeavours, and we are not lifted up, nor made forgetful of God by them, but keep humble and empty of self, and are more truly earnest to serve and please Christ, they prove the reality of grace in our hearts, and are means of advancing us in a Christian life, and in preparation for Heaven. Perhaps this is a meaning included by St. James, when he says, *let the brother of low degree glory in his exaltation.* When Christ deprived the Gergesenes of their herd of two thousand swine, he brought out a sad proof of their ignorance and worldly-mindedness; *the whole multitude of them besought him to depart from them.* They asked to get rid of Christ. Sad resolve! awful conclusion of His work among them! What can be more awful, or sadder to observe, than when one well-to-do, becoming impoverished, no uncommon thing in this land of business and commerce, gives up a profession of religion, whether much or little, becomes loose in conduct, takes perhaps to drinking, close as to all kindness for others in distress, and wholly absorbed, mind and heart, in the recovery of lost wealth. But if taking his losses properly to heart, as a check from his loving Saviour to worldliness of heart and conduct, he is humble, patient in faith and hope, diligent in his business, and truly Christian in his life and temper, how beautiful is it, how instructive, how explanatory of St. James' words, *let the rich glory in his being low, for as a flower of the grass shall he pass away.*

150.

In the churches epistle for St. Mark's day are these words, from the prophesy of Ezekiel: *They turned not when they went, but every one went straight forward.* How came it to be otherwise with St. Mark, if the same individual as John Mark, as is now generally concluded? For we read, that after attending Paul and Barnabas a little while in the work whereunto the Holy Ghost had taken them, *departing from them, he returned to Jerusalem. He went not with them to the work.* His misconduct gives rise to many reflections. I wish your attention to one. The influence of relations, either by word or example, sometimes leads young persons to a hasty profession of earnestness in religion. They have not looked into their own hearts. They have not earnestly and humbly sought the converting grace of the Holy Ghost. *Jesus said* to one who had offered to follow him, but showed a divided heart: *No man, putting his hand to the plough, and looking back, is fit for the kingdom of God.* Let John Mark's temporary fall (for he recovered, and by God's grace, became an eminent evangelist), warn all to examine into the causes and motives of their profession of religion. Was it from the advice and persuasion of others near and dear to you? or because their conversation and life seemed so blameless and upright? These, though good as moving influences, are not sufficient to fix the affections of the heart on God, and to keep the good thing taken up from such assaults of sin, the world and the Devil, as all Christ's soldiers will surely have. Let all consider well the message to the Church at Sardis: *I know thy works, that thou hast the name of being alive; and thou art dead. Be watchful and strengthen the things that remain which are ready to die. For I find not thy works full before my God.*

151.

Men may make an imitation of what is called the interior of Christianity, as well as of the exterior. There may be a semblance of inward joy in God, of love to Him and His precepts, of dependence upon Him, and filial reverence of Him, which is wrought by the power of fancy and the feelings on the soul, as characters in a play are brought on the stage, unreal, but very good imitations and life-like. Such christians, fetching their religion from pious books and sermons, or learning from others, of such and such signs of grace and evidences of salvation, and that they must have these to get to heaven, set themselves to work, so as to bring their faculties and senses to represent all these to themselves, and so being in the ways here spoken of, acquainted with those excellent and gracious affections and dispositions, and how they are outwardly shown, may excite them interiorly and exhibit them outwardly, which joined with some thoughts of Christ and God and divine things, will serve for an artificial piety to their own satisfaction and the commendation of others. Such religion is *of the earth, earthy:* and not that *new creature*, which, *if any man be in Christ*, he *is;* the effect of that converting grace which comes from heaven, and begets a divine life in the soul, of such supremacy and power, that as St. Paul says of it: *Old things are passed away, behold, all things are made new.* See then your need of that prayer. *Create a clean heart in me, O God, and renew a right spirit within my bowels.*

132.

In our contemplation of Mary, and the grace bestowed on her, for she was *full of grace*, we should not overlook the saintly excellencies of her espoused husband, Joseph. We need not examine into the Divine purposes in this espousal. Infinite wisdom ordered and arranged it. But we should not fail to observe and admire Joseph's submission to the Divine will, made known to him by an angel, trying as it would be to him, exposing him to the suspicions and contempt of his neighbours and the world. Observe his faith and courage in taking to him Mary as his wife; in his careful guardianship of her and the Divine Infant in the journey to Egypt and back; in his entire obedience to every direction and command of God. What wisdom, what piety, what graces did he give proof of? Let us endeavour to daily walk after him, and according to the work or trials God calls us to, to imitate blessed Joseph's exemplary conduct. It will ensure us the favour of Him, who though subject to Joseph as His foster-father, in the cottage of Nazareth, watched over him as the Incarnate God, and has now placed him in great nearness to Himself, among the saints, who for evermore encircle His throne in heaven.

153.

Some of you complain of distractions in prayer, and want of comfort, and that you have not recollection of spirit and tranquility of mind and heart at and after prayer. But consider if this may not be a merited chastisement of God for many past negligences and sins, and a just and merciful call to that self-humiliation before Him, which is ever pleasing to Him and profitable to ourselves. You admit that present chastisement from God is deserved by you, and will be both just and merciful; just because having often shut your heart against Him when He knocked at it by convictions of sin or duty, and calls to keep from the world's snares; it is just that now when you call on Him, He should seem to keep the door of His heart not so quickly or fully open as you wish. And surely such chastisement is merciful if you only view it, as light, compared with what you deserve. If God dealt with you according to your deserts, where would you now be? If we were more humble, we should never open our mouths to complain of any of God's dealings with us. And what greater fruit can we gather from prayer than a spirit of entire conformity to the will of God, and closer resemblance to our Saviour in His dereliction on the cross: *My God, My God* (He cried), *Why hast Thou forsaken me?* Was not all this according to God, His Father's will? Wait on God in faith and patience and submission. *Expect the Lord, do manfully, and let thy heart take courage, and wait thou for the Lord.*

184.

Are not two sparrows sold for a farthing? and not one of them shall fall to the ground without your Father. What comfort should we find in all our trials, what confidence and ease in our greatest afflictions and pressing calamities, if thoroughly convinced of this truth, as spoken by Christ for our peace of heart. If a son knew his father powerful, wise, wealthy, and tenderly loving of himself, what assurance would he have of his care and help in all his affairs and difficulties! With how much greater reason may we have a thorough confidence in the watchful providence of God our Father in Heaven. No tenderness nor affection can come near to that with which God regards us. We may rest satisfied that what He appoints or permits is for our greater good. The love He bears us in His Son, our Saviour Jesus Christ, will not let Him be backward to keep and bless those for whose sake he gave up that Son to the sufferings and ignominy of the cross. *He that spared not His own Son, but delivered Him up for us all, how hath He not also with Him given us all things. My father and my mother have left me, but* (the Psalmist finds his comfort in adding) *the Lord hath taken me up. The Lord ruleth me, and I shall want nothing. I am a beggar and poor, the Lord is careful for me.* If we only considered the fatherly providence of God as Holy Scripture in these and many more declarations brings before us, and the tender love which He has for us, how heartily should we cleave to and follow that Saviour Jesus, by whom alone any one can come to God as a Father.

155.

Jesus invites each of you to come to Him. Why will any of you delay and put off till to-morrow that giving of the heart to God which he calls for. You are conscious of sin, and doubtless have sorrows. For you is that invitation, *Come to me, all you that labour and are burdened, and I will refresh you.* And that promise, *him that cometh to me I will not cast out.* *I desire not the death of him that dieth saith the Lord God, return ye and live.* There is access to God now, by Christ; there may not always be; the *five foolish virgins who taking their lamps, did not take oil with them, were shut out* of the marriage. You call yourself a Catholic, and have the lamp of profession. Have you also the oil of the Holy Spirit's grace? Only Christ can give that to you, and if you are keeping back your heart from Him, through unbelief, love of this world and its empty pleasures, carelessness, sloth, a vain and deceptive purpose of being a better Christian by and by, or a yielding to some besetting temptation, you are holding your lamp without the oil that keeps its light alive. Take heed and do not longer grieve that heart of tender love which woos you to be *wise unto salvation. Take with you words, and return to the Lord, and say to him: take away all iniquity and receive the good, and we will render the calves of our lips:* the sacrifice of hearty prayer and praise. *We are made partakers of Christ: yet so, if we hold the beginning of His substance,* the life of grace within our souls, *firm unto the end.*

156.

Let me guard you against a dangerous error. Some professedly religious persons, wishing not to seem uncivil to the world by not complying with its customs and fashions, or unduly influenced by a care for their own case, reputation with their neighbours, emolument, or advancement in life, thus easily find a kind of side door, so to speak, to slip out into the world, mingle with it, and share in many of its questionable ways and wrong spirit. Though keeping up some regular service of Christ, in the exercise of some duties of religion, and avoiding such vices, as even men of the world brand with their condemnation, and considering themselves as having those characters which they learn from books or sermons to be marks of God's children; yet their case really is that spoken of by St. John: *They are of the world; therefore of the world they speak, and the world heareth them.* They are trying that impossible thing: to *serve two masters.* The world and the grace of God cannot lodge together, and form and shape out two districts in the soul of man. That grace, like a strong and living fire within us, will consume the whole body of death out of the affections and will, and *bring into captivity every understanding unto the obedience of Christ.* Like leaven, it will ferment the whole mass in which it is wrapped up, while that aim to keep well with the world, of which I would guard you, as *a little leaven corrupteth the whole lump* of the Christianity of those who do not resolutely watch and pray to keep fast that advice of the apostle: *Love not the world, nor the things which are in the world. If any man love the world, the charity of the Father is not in him.*

157.

There is another evil besides that spirit of conformity with the world of which I have before told you, that religious persons may easily fall into. Catholics have, perhaps, much reason to be apprized of this. It may be, that by a strong and becoming zeal against the opinions (for their religion is too often little else than opinion) of those who are not of their own Church, they overlook their own great sinfulness, and even their own guiltiness before God. Two apostles, one of them the loving John, would have *commanded fire from heaven* upon those whom they deemed Christ's enemies. *Jesus rebuked them, saying, you know not of what spirit you are.* True piety is like a mighty, but gentle heat, which cherished in the heart disperses a warm, but calm and quiet spirit, through the members of the body, not inflaming any with hot and feverish impulses. Like Aaron's serpent, which eat up the serpents of the Egyptian magicians, true Christian piety absorbs and swallows up passions and prejudices, which self, and not the grace of God, stirs up in us; while our Lord said to the Samaritan woman: *You adore that which you know not, we adore that which we know; for salvation is of the Jews,* so far from showing any hot zeal against the Samaritans, he again and again makes them the subjects of His commendation and examples of virtue and grace to the Jews, His own people. That religion which runs out into vehemence against others, whether expressed by our unkind actions or sour words, or kept and even cherished within us, as a temper of our minds does not come from heaven:

from that *God who is love*: *The Lord is sweet to all, and his tender mercies are over all his works.*

158.

Our Heavenly Father and God has given us this promise : *I will give my laws into their mind, and in their heart will I write them, and I will be their God, and they shall be my people.* Now God's promises are solemn covenant engagements, and sure of fulfilment, unless we wilfully cast them from us. The love of God, then, and of his holy will, and a willing, steadfast, hearty obedience to all His commandments is the mark and token of a true Christian. Let each of us often enquire within ourselves : Is it so with me ? Do I carefully and honestly seek by prayer, by much watchfulness, over myself, my feelings, my temptations, my calls of duty, that it may be so ? Do I keep the ear of my heart open to the whisperings of conscience enlightened by the word of God, and quickened by the Holy Spirit ? Do I get forward, as one who is under God's teaching, will, and dealings, will not fail to grow in grace and in the knowledge of the Lord and Saviour, Jesus Christ ? Am I ruling my life, not by maxims of human reason, nor by the likings of flesh and blood, nor by the customs of others, and the spirit and ways of the world around me, but by God's revealed precepts and truths ? Our minds and hearts are, too, like those of unruly and self-willed children, who want much restraint, and that it should neither be cast aside, nor much relaxed. If we would have God take and keep up His abode in us, and be to us our God, and we His people, let us fear God out of love, and not seem to love Him from fear.

159.

Observe attentively those words of St. Paul. *We know that to them that love God, all things work together unto good; to such as according to His purpose, are called to be saints.* All things; he makes no exception. When he makes none, make not you any. *Be strong in the grace which is in Christ Jesus;* give glory to God, and resolve with Job, although He should kill *me, I will trust in Him.* He may for a season seem to be your enemy, in order to become your eternal friend. After all your trials and anguish, you must conclude with David: *It is good for me that thou hast humbled me, that I may learn thy justifications.* God's glory is seen when he works by means; more seen, when he works without means; above all, when he works contrary to means. It was a great work for Christ to open the eyes of the blind; a greater to do it by applying clay and spittle; things more likely, seemingly, to take away, than restore sight. He sent an horror of great darkness on Abraham, when preparing to give him comforting light. He touched the hollow of Jacob's thigh and lamed him, when going to bless him. He smote Saul with blindness when intending to open the eyes of his mind, and make him an apostle and a saint. He refused the request of the woman of Canaan for awhile, but afterwards she obtained her desire. See therefore that *all the ways of the Lord are mercy and truth to them that seek after His covenant and His testimonies. Follow after holiness*, and in all your trials, hear Him saying : *I will not leave thee, neither forsake thee.*

160.

We shall make a great mistake, as to our personal religion, if we place it only in external compliance with the commandments of God. There is an outer, and an inner man. It is a superficial and deceptive profession of piety, which intermeddles only with the former. It storms and carries the outworks, but enters not into the strong fortress of the heart, defended by inward pride, self-will, earthly affections, envy, vain-glory, and many other evil dispositions, which, though driven out of our visible behaviour, by a fear of God's threats and some kind of regard to His promises, retreat and secure themselves in the inner man of our hearts, as a castle. We may not carry out our revenge for injuries into any act of offence to them, and yet not be willing to forgive those who have offended us; we may not cheat or take advantage of an ignorant or careless customer or employer, and yet love this world's wealth, and yet not *mind the things that are above, but the things that are upon the earth.* We may be unwilling to let our religion be too busy with our inward thoughts, passions and inclinations. And when our attachment to outward and worldly things begins to be cooled by satiety or age, or any other repressive cause, we may yet feed our inner self-love, by feelings of contempt for others, satisfaction at their inferiority, mistakes, or disappointments, and by contemplation of our own fancied superiority or attainments, wisdom, or wit, or any thing for which we are or have been well spoken or thought of. Against this great and dangerous error, let us keep in mind that we have to do with that God who says: *I am the Lord, who search the heart and prove the reins, to give to every one according to his way.*

161.

Let us remind ourselves again, that to be attacked by evil passion and thought, is a very different case from the being overcome by them. As long as we consent not, but reject the sin or evil suggested, not only with our reason but our will, there is no separation between our God and Father, and us. Some are much molested by evil thoughts, by which others, naturally, perhaps, of a more placid and composed spirit and less excitable temperament, are less troubled. Pride, vain-glory, hastiness of temper and speech, self-indulgence, sloth and other evils beset some more than other Christians. Yet the former may not at all consent to such temptations. They flee by prayer and faith, to Him who has vouchsafed to become their loving Heavenly Father; and to that Saviour with whom they have a blessed union, and probably advance more in spiritual life than those who are less tempted and tried. True holiness, after the image of Christ, is only attained through efforts and many struggles. Let none, then, be discouraged because of the violence or frequency of temptation; our Heavenly Father observes all we pass through, and never withdraws His love for us while we do not withdraw our hearts from Him.

162.

Men, far off from God, and in the tumult of the world, have found themselves drawn away from it, by the attraction of the Cross of Christ. It was so with St. Francis of Assisium, St. Ignatius Loyola, St. Francis Xavier, and many others who have been drawn by that Cross, to long for a new and better heart, and to lead a truer and nobler life; more worthy of a rational and immortal being. And as such came, by that way of the Cross, nearer to God, earthly things which had gratified them closely, began to lose their hold, more or less quickly. They failed to satisfy their awakened desires, and following on to know, they knew more of God. Their hearts more and more reached out to Christ, once crucified, now reigning in heaven, to be their Saviour and advocate with the Father, their Brother, Councillor, Friend, and God. Present joys became as passing shadows; sorrows came, but did not overpower, nor daunt; pain tried patience, but did not turn away from God. They kept on, knowing that Christ was leading and guiding, and though the cross was before them, and on them daily, yet heaven and its glorious rest behind, threw such radiance upon that Cross, that it was rather sought to than shrunk from. *God forbid* (writes St. Paul) *that I should glory, save in the cross of our Lord Jesus Christ, by whom the world is crucified to me, and I to the world*. But with how few of us is this the case! May it be so with all who hear or read what I have now brought before them.

Lord Jesus, when we stand afar,
   And gaze upon Thy holy Cross,
In love of Thee, and scorn of self,
   Oh! may we count the world as loss.

When we behold Thy bleeding wounds,
   And the rough way that Thou hast trod,
Make us to hate the love of sin,
   That lay so heavy on our God.

Give us an everlasting faith
   To gaze beyond the things we see;
And in the mystery of thy death,
   Draw us, and all men unto Thee.

www.ingramcontent.com/pod-product-compliance
Lightning Source LLC
Chambersburg PA
CBHW020308170426
43202CB00008B/540